"Ever struggled with the Psalms? A boring book of poetry? Unrelatable? Like you are just reading someone else's thoughts? What if the Psalms weren't meant to be distant and obscure but a manual on how to commune with God and observe His majesty? Gene Baillie's latest book brings the Psalms to life through a fascinating adventure. The Psalms are meant to be explored. They are meant to relate to and give us an understanding of the glory of the Lord. The *King's 19th Palace* breaks down the Psalms in a simple but elegant way to encourage the reader to rethink the Psalms and how he can learn and grow from them and, most importantly, meditate on how Christ the Cornerstone is ever present throughout the 19th Palace and every other book of Scripture. I love it!"

   — *Heath Rosenberger*, Anderson, SC
      Husband and father, lay-church teacher, sales executive

"Your book has stirred up in me a great desire to spend more time in the Psalms."

   — *Elsie Newell*, Anderson, SC
      Bible teacher of women, teenage girls, and grandchildren

"I am not good about thinking abstract, so this way of learning about the Psalms has been like a fresh breath of air to my brain. I will read again with Bible in hand to reference your details and application as I again explore the 'rooms' of the *King's 19th Palace*."

   — *Marcie Brown*, Casa Grande, AZ
      Christian, wife, mother, specialty baker

"The *King's 19th Palace* is a remarkable book of great spiritual power. I enjoyed the symbolism of each room correlating with how our lives are affected. The story displayed much emotion of sadness and joy."

   — *Mary Springer*, Omaha, NE
      Retired nurse

"Highly recommend this book . . . It is fascinating, engaging, evokes your imagination to a new level, and is very creative. Using a unique approach with autobiographical elements, the author factually states and applies solid biblical truths. You will be prompted to learn how your 'stone' can be built upon the 'Cornerstone' of Faith."
 — *Mark Chandler*, Seattle, WA
 Christian friend and encourager

"Dr. Baillie takes us on an unexpected journey . . . into the depths of the Psalms where we can meet Christ the Cornerstone and realize we are living stones . . . beside still waters where we are nourished and thus grow . . . . Into the din of war, as we watch the King of kings utterly reign over the enemy, we take courage . . . we sing songs of praise with angels . . . and cry tears of dread with David as he soaks his couch with tears. We are then led to a place where we remember the Lord is our hiding place. This is rich, life-giving truth and transformation as we place ourselves directly into the story God has written. But then there is a surprising turn of events! Dr. Baillie brings his family along on his journey through this one of the many palaces of God. I'm inspired to do the same. Who knew you could immerse yourself in the Word like this? You'll have to be still. You'll have to move on to meat and not be content with milk. But what a feast God provides! Thank you, Gene, for your testimony of what you have seen in God's Word. I can't wait to read this with my children!"
 — *Dr. Dale Treash*, Anderson, SC
 Pediatrician, friend, and fellow elder

"I love your book—it is *amazing*! Part of Mary in the book is me. For years we have begged you to write down your story. You have now written it . . . intertwined in HISstory. This is so 'you' . . . the man I grew up calling Daddy. Your story and song . . . every word is shouting His praise, showing your every step is on His directed path of righteousness for your good and *His* glory!
 — *Becky Baucum*, Clemson, SC
 Author's daughter

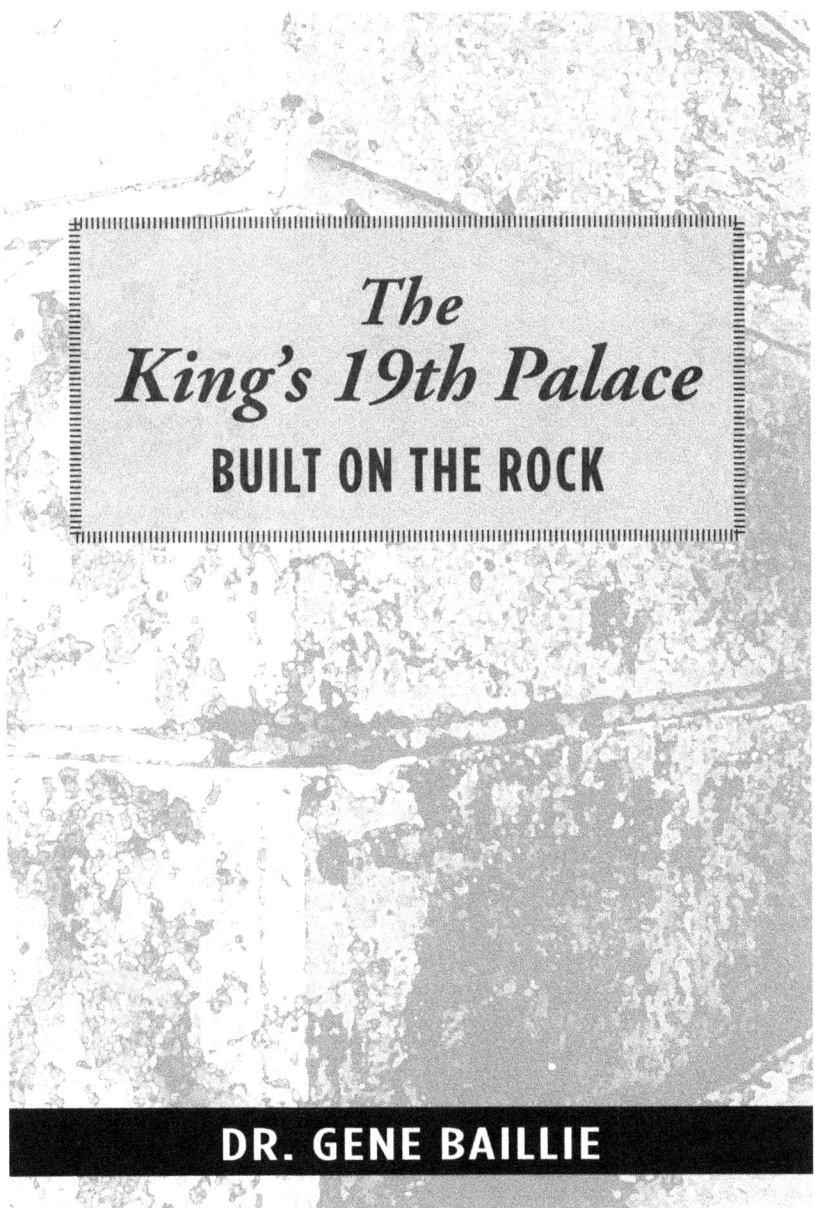

The King's 19th Palace
BUILT ON THE ROCK

DR. GENE BAILLIE

Gene Baillie Publishing, LLC

Copyright © 2023 Gene Baillie
Gene Baillie Publishing, LLC

All rights reserved. No part of this publication may be reproduced, stored in a retrieval system, or transmitted in any form or by any means—electronic, mechanical, photocopy, recording, scanning, or other—except for brief quotations in critical reviews or articles, without the prior written permission of the publisher.

The quoted ideas expressed in this book (but not Scripture verses) are not, in all cases, exact quotations, as some have been edited for clarity and brevity. In all cases, the author has attempted to maintain the speaker's original intent. In some cases, quoted material for this book was obtained from secondary sources, primarily print media. While every effort was made to ensure the accuracy of these sources, the accuracy cannot be guaranteed.

Unless noted otherwise, Scripture quotations are from the Holy Bible, English Standard Version (ESV), copyright © 2001 by Crossway Bibles, a publishing ministry of Good News Publishers. (This author capitalized the first letter of deity pronouns in ESV passages.)

Editing and composition assistance from Grant Rahme and Lisa Parnell
Cover design based on author's photograph of Western wall cornerstone
 in Jerusalem
Interior layout design and e-book by Lisa Parnell

ISBN 978-0-9964972-7-5 (paperback)
ISBN 978-0-9964972-8-2 (e-book)

Printed in United States of America

Preface

This book is dedicated to my King who is the triune God who has given me life and breath and all things, including the ability to read, understand, and apply His written Word to every aspect of my life. Starting each day with my Savior and Lord, I am being renewed as I read through the Bible each year, and I love the Psalms!

With the Lord's help and many others, I have written this book for those of my family and friends—present and future—who desire to explore the King's 19th palace (Psalms) and learn how their living stone is or can be built upon the Cornerstone.

Build *your* house on the Rock—not on sand. Christ the Cornerstone will help, leading you through the chaos of this worldly life and guiding you by His truth toward His promised and certain eternal life.

Chapter 1

I shook my head in disbelief at my strange new surroundings. I was in a different place altogether—I could tell from the pattern and texture of the rock. I pushed my palms against the cave wall where I guessed the opening had been, but it was solid rock. I had left my small backpack on the other side of this wall, but at least I still had my headlamp. I realized the light was not on, yet the space I now occupied was brightly lit. I could see it was a cavern of sorts, but I couldn't quite place the source of the light. It seemed as if the light emanated from the very atmosphere. So strange. I closed my eyes in the hope I would be able to orient myself, but when I opened them again, it had made no difference. In my mind I tried to retrace my steps, but still, I wasn't able to grasp how I had tumbled into this place of seemingly alternative reality. I kept retracing my steps mentally, and my mind kept on making good sense of everything I had experienced—right up to the point where I had stepped through the last opening.

Intrigued by a purple stone that looked like amethyst and was shaped like an obelisk, I attempted to remove it from the cave wall, which had evidently triggered the "door" in the cave wall to open. At that point my memory became hazy. I had twisted the amethyst crystal, which gave me access to this room, but as I stepped carefully through the opening, something strange happened. I lost all semblance of space, gravity, and time as my body hurtled through a kaleidoscope of light and color.

Experiencing a severe sense of vertigo as I stood up, my first thought—albeit with a smile on my face—was that I had fallen through some kind of wormhole into another dimension. How else could I explain the extreme disparity between this cavernous "room" and the previous two I had entered? Or was it a cave? It certainly looked like a cave, but it was bright, and I couldn't place the source of the light—it seemed ubiquitous. My heart pounded out a high-tempo drumroll, and I felt the hair on my arms and the nape of my neck rising. In spite of my confusion and concern, I felt a quick surge of regret. I had promised my wife I would call her tonight, but my cellphone was in my backpack on the other side of ... whatever "dimension" I had stumbled into. I tried to calm myself down, feeling genuinely afraid and unsure of what had just transpired. Why had I left my backpack? No food, only water. No phone, but would it work underground anyway?

I sat down on a protruding shelf of rock, which I realized was a carefully shaped stone bench. *What's happening to me? Where am I?* I had evidently stumbled upon a more convoluted and complex caving system than I first imagined. My immediate plan was to return to the surface, as I had on previous occasions, to where my campsite was set up in a cave just beyond a shallow overhang in the Shining Rock Wilderness. I had specifically taken some time from my busy schedule to be here in the Appalachian foothills, near the beautiful Blue Ridge Parkway about an hour from my home in Greenville, South Carolina.

My mind was desperately scrambling to process the puzzling series of events I had experienced over the past two hours. What started me on this journey of discovery was that tunnel linking the overhang to the cave. I settled myself more comfortably on the beautiful stone bench, trying to determine how such a well-crafted structure came to be carved into the wall of this room so deep inside a cave ... or was I really deep inside a cave? I had no idea! I cast my mind back to the previous morning. It was the third time I had traveled to explore this overhang in the foothills, and I still had not told anyone else about the cavelike opening or its location. As my mind drifted back in time, I remembered discovering some evidence at the entrance suggesting Cherokee Indians had been there: two small, flint-napped arrowheads and a hollow cane reed. I knew young Cherokee hunters used these reeds as blowguns to hunt squirrels and other small game.

I could tell the arrowheads were from another era, but I found no other evidence indicating any other humans had ever been there. By following the chronological pattern of my journey, I was hoping to find my return route to that overhang near the cave opening above the river. I allowed my mind to drift, and it quickly took me to yesterday's version of myself, sitting at my desk in my office. I began the process of slowly recalling the series of events that had brought me to this strange new place. Human memory is a fascinating phenomenon—I could almost taste the strong Columbian coffee I had been drinking at my computer.

I continued testing my memory, and it was suddenly flooded with all the bad things that had been brewing in our world the previous day. My focus is generally trained on the good news—I do my best to avoid visual or even audio clips regurgitating the world's bad news—but it's sometimes unavoidable. Via my iPhone, I am able to quickly read a summarized version of the latest encroachments against human freedom, and when I sift through the muck offered by our mainstream media, it is often worse than I can imagine.

War, famine, disease, drought, fires, flooding, and gross political overreach are the usual fodder served to those who swill at these troughs, but this time my mind perceived these threats differently. It seemed as if all these corrosive, worldly "toxins" had been drawn up into a syringe, and the needle was now poised, hovering over the upper arm of our collective human psyche. This was something I had to challenge head-on! Will my silence truly be construed as consent? Yes! So I stopped and looked to the heavens and said a silent prayer—at least I think I was looking up! My senses were assaulted by what I had seen and read over these past few months. I realized my mind was in turmoil. I was still reeling from having witnessed so much evil influence in our world—on just about every step of my life's journey—seeming to me to throttle life as we know it. I recognized something important in that moment: if humanity swept this current nonsense under the collective rug, it easily could muzzle us forever, not even allowing us a whispered whimper.

I'm not an important person in the grand scheme of things, just a church elder born and raised in a small town in Nebraska, now living in South Carolina. So how do I plan to even partially change such a wide-ranging global threat? None of us have the power to reverse what is coming, but each day I can choose to focus on being an influence for truth and good. I know God created all things, and I need to seek His guidance.

Am I dreaming? I asked my mind to do one more rewind to recall my first visit to this cave. My pickup had burbled smoothly beneath me as I repeatedly glanced at the forested hillside, not too far from a popular trail leading to the stunning rock made of quartzite in the Shining Rock Wilderness and Pisgah National Forest area of North Carolina. I have gone on a few hikes in this area, and I have fished from the banks of several trout streams. I had also heard reports claiming there are a number of small caves in this dense, forested wilderness, which immediately increased my attraction to the area. Besides above-ground hiking and fishing, I have had a passionate interest in cave exploration since childhood—one of my earliest memories is a visit to the Happy Jack chalk mine in Scotia, Nebraska, just 30 miles from my childhood home. I enjoy traveling, and since I now live in South Carolina for part of the year, I enjoy hiking and occasionally fishing in this remote, unpopulated, and well-preserved Shining Rock Wilderness. History tells us Daniel Boone traveled through this area, and the flint-tipped arrowheads I found at the cave also point to native Americans having occupied this exquisite landscape.

This was on my first trip to the area—I was on an off-trail hike in this rugged wilderness, and knowing twilight was approaching, I began looking for a place to camp overnight, hopefully away from bears and weather elements. I soon spotted a small indention on a hillside, but it didn't look like a cave at all—in fact, at first glance it seemed quite shallow. I needed a place quickly, however, to avoid the driving rain from a sudden mountain squall that had developed. I felt deflated, but when I drew closer to the overhang, it was larger than I had previously thought. I gratefully slid the backpack from my shoulders, feeling relieved to be out of the cold rain. I pulled a thick sweater and a pair of fleece sweatpants from my backpack to replace the drenched T shirt and jeans I was wearing. Feeling more relaxed and comfortable, I started exploring.

It wasn't long before I saw a small opening, hidden to one side of the shelf of rock. I strapped on my headlamp, and my excitement surged as I realized I was able to squeeze into the opening without much difficulty. The constricted channel of rock opened suddenly into a broad cave. After I had walked a few paces, taking a quick look around, I was unable to find any dry wood to make a fire, so I went back out to the overhang to retrieve my backpack. I traversed the constricted channel of rock again and rolled out my sleeping bag, thankful to be warm and dry, completely out of the elements. As I drifted into a peaceful sleep, I could hear the sound of water burbling through the rocks nearby, which I surmised was an underground river. The next morning I wanted to further explore the cave, but my time was limited, as I had business to attend to back in town. I loved the thought of possibly being the first person ever to venture into this cave. So far I had not seen evidence of any previous visitor, only the few telltale signs outside, suggesting native

Americans had likely sheltered under the overhang at some point in the history of this landscape.

Although I was grateful to have found shelter from the squall that drove me to this cave, I had not planned to spend the night in this wilderness. I'm always prepared for any emergency, of course, so I could actually have spent a few nights out, but I had a late-afternoon meeting that day. So I took one last look around the cave before grudgingly squirming through the rock channel to the overhang outside. Reviewing my GPS data, I could see where I had parked my truck some five miles away behind a dense thicket just off the gravel road. Using my GPS and a newly installed trails app on my iPhone, I began recording my route back. I hoisted my backpack onto my shoulders and struck out on a path across country, going through the intensely thick underbrush away from the overhang and this hidden cave.

On my second visit a few months later, I found two arrowheads and the hollow cane reed, as well as hearing and suspecting an underground river. On reaching the overhang I took some time to scout it more carefully, thinking there may be another opening into the caving system I knew was buried behind the cliff. The arrowheads were lying near one another deep under the overhang, and the reed was leaning against the rock face a few feet away. Feeling pleased with my find, I squeezed through the rock channel and entered the cave behind the overhang. Having more time to explore on that early sunny morning, I was eager to find the water I heard burbling on my first visit.

Finding the river was much easier than I had anticipated. I followed the sound of the running water, which grew louder as I approached the far end of the cave. It seemed to be coming from somewhere below the cave I was in, so I shined my flashlight over the edge of a shelf of rock, and there it was—an underground river reflecting the light back at me. I followed the river with my lamp, realizing it must have cut a narrow tunnel through the rock over the course of time. The tunnel was much wider than the river, so I guessed the water had probably been flowing more powerfully at previous times in its history. I was excited at my find, and really keen to explore this lower tunnel carved out by the river. I decided, however, to put that exploration on hold for the time being—no one knew where I was.

In case I ran into trouble on any journey, I had at least mapped my route to this cave using my trail app, but had forgotten to share this data with my family. After finding the underground river, I opened a can of baked beans, eating them cold with a slice of bread. I remember feeling elated, having achieved my objective of finding the source of water I had heard on my initial visit to the cave. I sang a song of gratitude to God for this entire place I had discovered, from which I would be able to continue the adventure I had begun. Similar to descending into a cave, I had a strong sense God was calling me to a deeper spiritual work He had set before me, so this cave seemed somehow related to that purpose for my life. As a Christian I feed on both physical and spiritual food, constantly aware of being an alien and stranger on earth—as believers we are called to be "in" the world but with the clear recognition we are not to be "of" this world. It is my daily custom to pray and read the truth God has set out for us in the Bible, after which I seek how He might use me that day to apply what I have read and learned.

On my third visit to the cave, I had brought sufficient supplies to spend a few days exploring, hoping to follow the underground river deeper into the suspected network of underground caverns I might find. I had arrived in the late afternoon and quickly built a small fire inside the cave beyond the overhang. Flickering firelight from my little campfire sent a spray of light and shadow dancing across the cave roof. As I watched this mesmerizing display, my eyes were drawn to the far end of the cave where I had found the shelf of rock above the underground river. I ran my eyes along the cavern ceiling toward the far end of the tunnel, but there was no visible cave roof at the farthest point. I was intrigued, realizing the tunnel roof must be a lot higher as it continued beyond this part of the cave. As excited as I was, I fell asleep quickly.

The next morning I rose early, grabbed my flashlight, took a swig of water from the bottle on my belt, then set out to explore the far end of the tunnel. I started following the passage, picking my way carefully through the rocks littering the floor, sometimes quite near to the river flow. I reached what I had initially thought was the end of the cave, but my beam of light revealed a sharp twist in the rock face, directly below the point I had expected to see the cave roof. I turned my face to the ceiling, and far above me, about three stories high, I saw the expansive cave roof. I lowered my eyes again, feeling a mixture of intrigue and elation. The river continued flowing through the tunnel, veering to the right. As I followed my light, the tunnel twisted and turned, becoming narrow at times but then broadening out as I continued. At one point I had to squeeze through a sharp turn to the left, and when I emerged through the gap, it seemed as though I had just gone through a door. I found myself in an exquisite, high-domed room with glittering crystals visible everywhere.

I felt like Gimli the Dwarf might feel after finding a fresh goldmine. I started exploring this crystal room, reverently approaching one gleaming, purple crystal embedded shoulder-high in the midst of all the quartzite rock. *Could this be amethyst?* I wondered. I knew amethyst was indeed present about 150 miles away—I had also seen it in Arizona—and also in the largest amethyst cave in the world (Crystal Castle near Byron Bay in Australia). But I had never heard of amethyst being found in the Appalachian foothills. I tried to pry it loose by applying pressure, turning it first to the left then the right, when suddenly I heard the eerie sound of rock grating on rock. My first terrified thought was that the cave walls were collapsing. I quickly hunkered down in fright, covering my head with my hands, but after a few seconds the sound stopped. I looked up and immediately realized I was looking into another "room." The rock wall had slid open to reveal what appeared to be another rocky chamber. I instinctively narrowed my eyes against the bright, radiant source of light emanating from the chamber—a chamber I had expected to be hidden in deep darkness. I stood in awe at the new entrance that had been revealed, wondering how many more caves I would find.

My heartbeat picked up pace as I considered this new development. Had I simply stumbled upon a previously unexplored cave, or had I found an entirely new caving system? I studied the new "doorway," realizing the grating sound I heard was a portion of the cave wall to the right of the crystal sliding to reveal the rocky room before me.

This led me to assume I was perhaps instrumental in this unexpected development—by putting pressure on the crystal or turning it when trying to pry it loose from the rock, I must have triggered some preset mechanism to slide the door open. It reminded me of movie scenes like in *Raiders of the Lost Ark*. I thought I had turned the crystal first to the left, but only when I had turned it to the right—in my attempt to pry it loose—did the grating sound begin.

To test my theory, I once again applied pressure to the crystal, but this time turning it to the left. Sure enough, the wall started sliding in the opposite direction, shutting off the entrance to the new room I had discovered. The same horrible noise grated across my nerves as the wall slid slowly to the left, cutting off the source of the radiant glow emanating from behind the wall. I looked carefully to see where the two walls joined, but there were no telltale signs, not even a hairline crack. Thrilled at my discovery, I opened the door again, and this time I stepped across the threshold, not giving a second thought to the nagging premonition I felt about the unexpected light pushing back the darkness.

Expecting my foot to land upon solid rock was my first mistake. As I stepped across the threshold, I experienced a falling sensation . . . but not quite! Rather, I seemed to be tumbling, weightless, through space, and my vision blurred into a pinwheel of light and color. I remember feeling panicked as I clutched desperately at the air around me hoping to find a solid surface. I also recall the sound of water sloshing around in the bottle on my belt.

So here I sit, and try as I might, I am unable to fill the missing gap in my memory between the sound of water sloshing and me shaking my head in disbelief at my strange new surroundings. I am sitting on a low parapet wall, which was masterfully carved into a bench, contemplating my next step. I rise from the stone bench and begin to explore the room in detail. I choose a random spot on the cave wall and push my palms against it in a futile attempt to find the opening again. The wall does not give an inch—it's solid rock.

Chapter 2

You are God's building or temple in which His Spirit dwells, built on His firm foundation. He has trained you to build up others on the foundation of His Son (based on 1 Corinthians 3:9–14).

Despite being unable to find the opening through which I entered this cave of light, I am at peace. The soft light permeating the atmosphere has a soothing effect that immediately disables any sense of panic trying to rise within me. It's as if the light helps me to regain the upper hand every time my mind plunges into the dark abyss of thoughts grappling for my attention: *This is it, Gene. This is where you die! No food and no exit. Even if Carol could use the tracking data to find the overhang, how will anyone replicate my movements through these cave walls? No, buddy, just face it. You're done!* I sense my face has contorted into a worried grimace, but as I raise my eyes, the light bathes the frown from my face and suffuses my being with peace again. I also sense there will be a way out, and I'm certain my adventure has only just begun.

My search for an opening along the length of the near wall has been futile, so I return to the stone bench to consider my next move. Sitting on the shelf of rock, I say a prayer as I lean back against the wall and close my eyes. My prayer is specific. I first thank the Father in all circumstances and for always directing my every step in life, giving me the ability and also the will to try to accomplish every task He has set before me. I ask His protection over my family while I am away and for my own safety on this journey of exploration and discovery. I don't ask for a way out of my predicament; I simply ask for God's Spirit to reveal to me the next step I must take. I feel the bright light permeating and surrounding me through my closed eyelids, and as I soak up the radiance, an image appears in my mind. The cave I am in has become a construction site, pared down to the bedrock foundation. Rising from the bedrock is a massive cornerstone with a central area of seemingly connected arch and capstone.

I see myself approaching the cornerstone, and I marvel at the smooth-grained texture of the granite. The stone is almost as tall as I am, and I have to stand on the tips of my toes to see the flat-top surface. I run my fingers along the granite as I walk around the stone, which appears to be as wide as it is tall. It is cool to my touch. As I turn the third corner, I see an inscription on the stone at eye level, but I am unable to read it—the characters of the script seem to be letters etched from the Hebrew alphabet. I remember reading about how ancient cultures inscribed pertinent details on the cornerstone of an important building to indicate the names of the architect and the builder as well as the date of construction. Using this rudimentary knowledge, I apply it to the script, but it seems the architect and builder are the same person, and I am unable to comprehend the date of construction. (I now know it was letters and not numbers: *Bereshit bara Elohim,* meaning "Beginning God created.")

My heart leaps for joy as I sit contemplating this vision or dream because the image brings to mind a Scripture referencing the Jewish Messiah as the cornerstone, sometimes referenced as the capstone. I love the book of Psalms, so I know this portion from Psalm 118:19–22 well—I have committed it to memory:

> Open to me the gates of righteousness, that I may enter through them and give thanks to the Lord.

> This is the gate of the Lord; the righteous shall enter through it. I thank you that you have answered me and have become my salvation. The stone that the builders rejected has become the cornerstone.

My excitement builds as I recite the passage out loud. This is the gate of the Lord! *What are you trying to tell me through your Spirit? I know You have changed me, so I am definitely among the righteous who by Your Spirit can enter through this gate. I recognize the cornerstone as a symbol of Your Son, Christ the Messiah, but how does this lead me to the next step I must take?* I anxiously wait for some form of response to my silent prayer, and I open my eyes, struck with strange disappointment at the stone's disappearance. Another excerpt of Scripture flashes through my mind, where Peter references Jesus as a living stone rejected by men, and my spirit leads my slower human mind to follow the logical steps being laid out. I know I'm on the brink of something important, so I take a deep breath and close my eyes again. I bring to the forefront of my mind words from 1 Peter 2:

> As you come to him, a living stone rejected by men but in the sight of God chosen and precious, *you yourselves like living stones* are being built up as a spiritual house, to be a holy priesthood, to offer spiritual sacrifices acceptable to God through Jesus Christ.[1]

That's it! I have the answer. Christ is the Cornerstone, and I am a living stone. I am an integral part of the spiritual house God is building. I am one of the crucial blocks of living stone populating God's palatial Kingdom—I simply have to seek my rightful place. Carrying the image of the Cornerstone in my mind, I start at the far end of the wall from which the stone bench is carved. I step up

---

1. 1 Peter 2:4–5, my emphasis

The King's 19th Palace

onto the bench and place both palms against the wall, moving to my left and shifting my palms along the wall as I go.

I repeat the process step by step, singing a song of praise while I work my way across the length of the wall. When I reach a point about two-thirds of the way along the wall, something happens. I feel a strange heat emanating from the wall, and between my hands I see an inscription becoming visible. I keep my hands steady while the characters complete their form. Yet again the writing appears to be made up of Hebrew symbols, and they shimmer with the same radiant light that fills the cavern. I remove my palms from the wall, and the letters remain visible, pulsating with light. I take a deep breath, then I place the palm of my right hand over the newly formed symbols. I experience an inexplicable sensation, as if my hand is melding with the wall. My arm vibrates gently in resonance with the contact of my palm against the wall, and I hear the soft sound of voices lifted up in song: "Blessed is he who comes in the name of the Lord! We bless you from the house of the Lord. The Lord is God, and He has made His light to shine upon us."[2] *Am I in some kind of house?*

Ephesians 2 teaches us we were dead in our sins, unable to save ourselves, but God our King, through His great love and mercy, made us alive through His Son. By His grace we have been saved, through faith—not by anything we have done or by any of our own work, but rather as His gift to us. The message of this "room" ends with words telling us we are fellow citizens and members of His house (as adopted children), being built on the foundation, with Jesus Christ as the Cornerstone and as the Capstone. He holds us together, joined together with all believers, creating that temple where His Spirit also dwells, teaching us His truth individually and together.

---

2. Psalm 118:26–27

Chapter 3

Keep on walking the narrow way leading to life and the source of Living Water. He teaches you to be a fisher of men (based on Matthew 7:14; Revelation 7:17; and Mark 1:17).

In the soft breeze, the lush green vegetation along the riverbank carried a rich and fecund scent of vitality. It was a smell I associated with fresh spring mornings, those dew-pearled mornings when life rises strong within the human heart. The early morning sun sparkled across the surface of the water, and I had a sense this would be a special day. I swished my trout line back and forth until I had sufficient length to reach my mark, releasing the hairy fly with a final downward flick of my wrist. My lure slid into the water directly beneath an overhanging bough near the far bank. I was below the rock overhang that led to the caves I had been exploring. I would sleep in that first cave again tonight, and hopefully cook a couple of rainbow trout over the embers of my fire. I retrieved my line in short static jerks, replicating the jagged movement of an insect swimming near the surface.

Fishing enables me to process life's everyday joys and struggles without much conscious effort. As I stood flicking my line through the plant-scented air then retrieving my lure, I entered a dreamlike state of contemplation. I had been forced to choose a path on my way to this location, and now that image sprang to mind yet again. To my left the path had extended into what appeared to be a rocky, more open landscape. The path was broad and seemed to be well traveled, and while there probably *were* some trails that led back to the river, I was unable to see any. To my right the path was narrow and heavily overgrown with thickets and vines, but I sensed it led directly to the river. Logic told me to take the broad pathway, but my heart told me to stick as close to the river as I could, choosing to put up with any inconvenience in my search for a special fishing spot.

My route to the river had involved yet another choice. To the left I saw a huge tree without any leaves. It had lost most of its bark, and I could tell it had been dead for some time. To my right, about 350 yards away, I saw another huge tree breaking through the canopy of trees along the riverbed. It had new green leaves shining brightly in the morning sun, and it radiated good health. I took this as a sign, so in spite of the seemingly difficult trail that followed the river, I began picking my way through the vegetation growing along the path. As I followed the trail that mirrored the contour of the river, the going became easier, with fewer obstructions. I also was given glimpses of the river as I walked, which greatly encouraged me.

I smiled now at this memory, happy my choice had led me to find this beautiful fishing spot. I flicked my line through the air, and I could feel the city stress melting away.

On my third cast, I landed a small brown trout, but it was below regulation size, so I slipped it back into the swirling water. Having achieved this minor victory, my old friend Murphy decided it was time to pay me a visit. My very next cast snagged something solid, and from the arc of my line, I could tell I had probably hooked a log on the riverbed. Feeling loathe to lose this particular fly I had spent more than an hour creating, I decided to strip down to my swimming suit and started wading in to retrieve the fly. After I took a few steps, the riverbed fell away suddenly, so I was forced to dive into the clear depths to retrieve my fly. It was caught on a large tree trunk on the riverbed, lodged among the rocks. My tugging had embedded it more deeply, so I struggled to release the hook on my first dive. I rose to the surface, filled my lungs with clean air and went down once more to loosen the precious dry-fly I had tied the week before.

Approaching the fly from a different angle on my second dive, I saw bright shafts of sunlight filtering through the slow-moving water. The light shone through the depths, and as I reached my hook, I saw a huge fish swimming swiftly toward the far bank where I had been casting. I watched as the fish reached the bank, but then it seemed as if it kept on swimming directly through what I thought was the riverbank. Mesmerized by the disappearing fish, I forgot my hook momentarily and started swimming after the fish. On reaching the bank, I realized the fish had led me to an underwater grotto that must have been fairly big because I could no longer see the fish. Excitement bubbled up inside of me—I knew I had to explore this new world. I rose to the surface once more before going back to retrieve my hook, then I sat on a rock in the sun, contemplating my next move. Caution warned me to return with a friend before exploring an underwater cave. Curiosity, however, urged me to have a quick look, just so I could evaluate the scope of this intriguing scene. It wasn't much of a struggle—curiosity won.

I grabbed my headlamp, stashed my fishing tackle, backpack, and clothes in a thicket of flowering bushes, then waded back into the river. When I was directly below the thick overhanging branch I had been casting toward, I took a deep breath and dove into the river's depths. The shafts of sunlight were much brighter now, and I could clearly see a large opening in the rocky riverbank about a foot above the riverbed. I swam through cautiously, holding onto the rocks as I pushed my way deeper into the grotto. I reached a point where the shafts of sunlight no longer penetrated the water, so I switched on my newly acquired water-resistant headlamp. The powerful beam immediately illuminated a rock wall about twelve feet ahead of me studded with clear quartz crystals. I figured I would have enough breath to touch the wall before returning to the surface, so I swam on.

When I reached the wall, I began tracing the crystals with my fingers, and as I moved up along the rock face, my head suddenly cleared water. As I scanned the cavern area with my light, I realized I had probably found a chamber somehow connected to the series of caves I had explored. I dove again and made a mental note of the exact spot I had surfaced, so I would know how to find my way back to the river. From the cave side, it was clear I had traversed a tunnel of rock from the river to this cave, and my bright light revealed the tunnel's width was about four feet, which narrowed appreciably toward the riverside opening. As I was turning back to the rock wall behind me, I saw the massive brown trout that had led me to this spot. He swam lazily now and seemed to be smiling as he headed back through the rock tunnel. I smiled back and thanked him before hoisting myself above water, up onto the ledge of rock above the crystal-studded wall.

What an adventure. It was barely 9:00 a.m. and here I was in an underground cave I had found by following a fish! I pondered the significance of the fish as a symbol, now recognizing I may well have been led here to search for more spiritual answers. Perhaps it hadn't been old Murphy who was involved in snagging my hook after all. With a newfound reverence for the rock on which I sat, I swung my feet out of the water, stood up, and began exploring my surroundings. The ledge on which I now stood led to a shallow chamber that, upon further scrutiny, turned out to be an antechamber. I first sensed this when I realized it was not my headlamp revealing the path before me, but rather a soft light emanating from a much larger chamber ahead. I switched off my headlamp, and as my eyes adjusted to the softer glow, I was struck by the sheer volume of the chamber I had entered. The smaller chamber opened up suddenly, giving me the impression of crossing over into a huge and grand entryway. A stone staircase rose before me, and I could see clearly now how the soft light at the top of the staircase spilled into the chamber below.

My bare feet whispered as I climbed the stairs, but as I neared the top, the hushed silence around me gave way to the sound of a song. I was reminded of the soft voices I heard lifted up in song on my previous visit to this caving system. Now, as I listened to what must surely be an "angelic" choir, my heart began to beat faster.

As I had felt on my first visit, I sensed a gentle, loving, awe-inspiring presence that increased the reverence I felt at the water's edge. At the top of the staircase was an open archway leading into a big room filled with the same resplendent brilliance I had experienced in the room with the stone bench. If I had been wearing shoes, I would have taken them off before entering. Standing beneath the arched entrance to the room in my swimming trunks, I felt underdressed as I closed my eyes and said a silent prayer of thanks for being guided to this empyrean[3] location.

I entered the room, and the words of the song now rang clearly, rising to the vaulted ceiling. I *knew* these words! I listened more carefully, and as I began to connect the words, letters written in light began to be displayed on the far wall. This time, though, the letters were scribed in English. The song seemed attuned to my mind because, as I began reading the first line of the scrolling letters on the wall, the choir sang the same words. Then, however, I skipped ahead, and as I did so, the song adjusted to reflect the new words I was reading. I started reading the first line again, and immediately the ethereal choir started singing in tandem with the words on which my eyes were focused. The words suggested I should keep walking the path I was on, offering the view that the man who

---

3. Heavenly; celestial

walks the wrong path will not be blessed and his life choices will deliver to him the result of his wrong choices. My mind went back to the fork in the path and the choice I had made to stay close to the river.

I had read these words many times before, yet, now, seeing them written in light and hearing them sung by seemingly angelic beings who were somehow in tune with my every thought, they came alive in my heart. I recognized the theme of progression—sensing some sort of reality instead of dream, even seeing somehow—I noted how a person is first drawn to walking with the wicked, then tempted to stand with sinners, and finally, taking a seat with scoffers. Each successive stage on this journey was leading toward an area of darkness seemingly separated from this room. It revealed to me how people become progressively entrenched in wrongful ways of living. By the time a man is seated among a crowd of people who are filled with scorn and mockery, that man is quickly attuned and diverted to their wrong and overarching ideology. He becomes one of the crowd, sometimes even vilifying others to prove he belongs. It was a sobering moment. I examined my own life, wondering if I, too, would be found wanting when the value of my existence was weighed in the balance.

I realized the choir had stopped singing while I contemplated the relevance of these words to my life. I continued reading, and the angelic voices immediately echoed the written words reflecting on my retinas. The man in question, the one who refuses to walk, stand, or sit with those who will lead him astray, this man is blessed! He is blessed because he meditates on the words I see written in light—these words, much like individual stones, make up the entire house the Master Builder constructed. That's when the penny dropped. The song I heard on my previous visit to this realm—whether a subterranean caving system or some kind of metaphysical reality reflecting ultimate Truth—was a means of audibly conveying the truth encapsulated within that specific room. I had a strong sense

I had only just scratched the surface of this reality, this Truth. The grand staircase gave me a sense I was in the entry room of quite a large, even a palatial structure—I reasoned I would find many more "rooms" encapsulating many more "songs."

Whether by revelation or through intuition, I knew these songs, or the words from which the songs were comprised, would be heard or seen in each of the cavelike rooms I would still visit; they were being sung or read perpetually through time. The only necessary component to complete the equation was a living being like myself to interact with what was being projected—a living stone who could meld with the walls of this constructed reality to become a part of the process and be a part of the actual building! A vibrant, living stone who could easily be integrated into this Kingdom of life and light. I also recognized another important aspect of this assimilation process: it would enable me and other living stones to reflect the energizing radiance of the house being built so the house could attract more stones. These new stones would in turn be integrated into the building to spread a brighter reflected Light into further reaches of the world. I can't really tell you how all these words, songs of praise, and unfolding events were so real and evident in my mind and heart.

I continued hearing as I was also reading, visualizing, and experiencing. I see this man, this living stone who is blessed because of the choices he makes, he will be like a transplanted tree beside living waters, which provide him nourishment. He is to follow a certain path, a certain way of living expressed throughout all of the rooms and houses, and throughout this entire Kingdom—essentially, he is to follow this directed path throughout his life. I perceive this huge room is like a summary and introduction to this palace and beyond.

I want to be such a man! Right now I will stay in this room filled with radiant light, and I will read these words again, probably several times, before proceeding to the other rooms. I know there are more rooms to explore—to observe, read, and apply to my life.

Furthermore, I believe I have found the key to moving between the rooms of this house. I plan to put my newfound knowledge to the test tomorrow. I will go back to that central chamber with the stone bench, where I can meld my being with the walls of the palace, giving me access to all the different rooms. It is my desire to learn as much as I can from all of the rooms. The choir had gone silent during my cogitation, but it started up again when I read and also sing along with the final verses being projected onto the wall. If I choose to walk the path of a blessed man who meditates on the words written in light, the Master Builder will know me; yet if I choose the way of the wicked, I will surely perish.

The room grew silent. I had read these verses many times before, but never had they gripped me with this sense of urgency. I wanted the Architect and Builder of this Kingdom to know me. I had no desire to perish. I was enveloped with a peace I was unable to comprehend with my mind, but my heart knew the source. I said a prayer of thanks, and I turned back to the staircase. Once I had descended the stairs, the radiance faded behind me, and I switched my headlamp on again. I found my spot on the ledge above the water, and now I dove into the pool below, quickly finding the tunnel that took me back to the river. The sun was about to set when I broke the surface of the water, and I marveled at how quickly time had passed while I had been meditating on the words written in light. What had felt like a few minutes in the awe-inspiring Presence had actually been closer to nine hours.

I collected firewood on my way up to the overhang and started a fire in the cave beyond. I ate my ready-made meal warmed up on the coals and quickly fell asleep, thrilled at the thought of what I had experienced, and what lay ahead of me on this journey of discovery.

Chapter 4

This is the day the Lord has made. Let us rejoice and be glad in it. Psalm 118:24

You know that thrill when you begin to wake—when your mind leaves the dreaming and is slowly gaining traction over its conscious thought process—and you are suddenly inundated with joy at what the day holds for you? This is how I started my day.

I stretched luxuriously in my sleeping bag, yawning contentedly. I lay there for a few moments and contemplated how I would go about testing my theory of intercavern travel. I wanted to draw closer to the Architect and Builder of this Kingdom I had discovered, knowing He was asking me to pay close attention—through detailed observation—while He is in the process of revealing to me the part I must play in His overarching plan. I added kindling to the coals still smoldering in my fire circle, and by the time I packed my knapsack, I had sufficient flame to boil some water. After eating a power bar and drinking a cup of coffee, I grabbed my daypack and followed the underground river to the high-domed cave filled with glittering crystals. As I approached the glimmering, purple crystal embedded in the quartzite rock, I had a sudden sense I was rushing something important. My focus had been so keenly trained on opening the door to the cave of light—and to search for more caves in the system I was exploring—I had neglected to marvel at the beauty surrounding me.

We so easily become inured to the wonders of our world, especially when we focus on the potential of experiencing *future* joy, rather than absorbing the joy eluding us *in the current moment*. I dropped my knapsack at the base of the stone-studded wall, lifted my eyes to the roof of the cave, and recaptured the breathless wonder I felt on my first visit to this dazzling place. I made a decision to stay present in the moment as I progressed through the different rooms I was hoping to find, irrespective of how exciting or enticing the next room might seem. After regaining my sense of wonder and amazement, I slung my daypack onto my shoulders, raised my right arm, and twisted the amethyst crystal to the right. The eerie sound of grating rock was followed by a burst of soft light spilling out through the open doorway.

I entered the cavern of light cautiously, first placing my left foot across the threshold. I gathered my resolve, feeling slightly trepidatious, wondering whether I would experience the same sensation of tumbling through space again, as I had on my first foray into this Kingdom that bridged two worlds. I closed my eyes and swung my right foot across the divide. Nothing happened. No sensation of tumbling weightless through space, no pinwheel of light and color blurring my vision. Instead, the door slowly closed behind me, making the same gritty, crunching noise as it sealed me into the chamber of light. I felt a bit deflated but also somewhat relieved. I certainly was expecting the disoriented confusion my initial entrance created. I began to wonder if this mystical landscape was simply responding to the level of experience I had accrued in this realm. Was I being spared the mystery and drama of my first visit now that I knew how to move between the walls? I still had so much to learn, but I knew a lot more than I did when I first took shelter under the overhang those many weeks ago. I think I am going beyond just detailed facts and gaining some understanding.

These thoughts encouraged me, so I walked briskly across the room to the stone bench carved into the far wall. I stepped up onto the bench about two-thirds of the way along the wall where I previously saw an inscription revealed, which seemed to be the key to the next room. Starting slightly to the right of where I gained entrance before, I placed both palms against the wall, moving to my left and shifting my palms along the wall as I walked. In a matter of seconds, I felt that strange heat emanating from the wall, and between my hands I saw the same inscription becoming visible. I held my hands steady while the pulsing characters completed their form and the Hebrew symbols appeared. The shimmering letters pulsed vibrantly with soft light as I placed the palm of my right hand over the glowing symbols. My arm began to vibrate gently as my hand started melding with the wall, and yet again I heard the soft sound of voices lifted up in song: "Blessed is he who comes in the name of the Lord! We bless you from the house of the Lord. The Lord is God, and He has made His light to shine upon us."[4] A shout of victory escaped me, and I laughed joyfully at my success. I was back in the house of the Lord!

I listened to the angelic choir singing the words of this favorite psalm, but I was not drawn to enter this room—at least not yet. A still, inner voice prompted me to keep searching the wall for another inscription, another key. Earlier in the morning, during those hazy moments between sleep and waking, I was filled with excitement at the thought of how I would start experimenting with the different possible means of access I had perceived for gaining entrance to the many buildings and rooms just waiting to be explored. Was it only by feelings or touch? I couldn't see any prominent crystals studding the wall, so I continued my search by placing both palms against the wall, moving to my left and shifting my palms along the wall as I walked. Growing quickly attuned to the process of finding a

---

4. Psalm 118:26–27

The King's 19th Palace

new key, I stopped when the rock wall became hot to my touch. I watched, fascinated, as yet another glowing inscription was revealed between my palms. Placing the palm of my right hand over the Hebrew symbols, my hand started melding with the wall, and I heard the sound of voices rising in song: "Why do the nations rage and the peoples plot in vain?"[5]

My heart accelerated wildly as I suddenly became aware of a room where intense action was unfolding before me. The room opened onto a broad balcony, and I caught the occasional glimpse of a fierce battle raging below, just beyond the Kingdom wall. I watched in amazement for a quick moment through the twelve-inch portal that had opened under my palm, and I knew this was a room I somehow *had* to explore! As soon as I made this decision, the portal stretched out into an oval doorway that I could enter.

I took a deep breath and crossed over into the room. Before me a large wooden desk blocked my path to the balcony, so I skirted its edge, hoping to see more of the battle action I had glimpsed beyond the wall. When I reached the corner of the desk, I became aware of a pair of virtual-reality glasses perched on the desk, arms open, as if inviting me to put them on. I picked them up, noticing how opaque the lenses were, but when the glasses covered my eyes, I froze in terror, for I had been translated into the midst of the battle.

The sky was thick with falling arrows, and the mighty roar of war all around me shook me to my core . . . until I realized I was merely an observer. None of the soldiers paid any attention to me, and one of the arrows I was unable to avoid passed right through me—as if it or I were a hologram. Shaken but relieved to be alive, I began to relax, tuning in to the conversations taking place among what appeared to be an elite class of officers. It seemed as if all the nations of the earth were gathered together at the wall, plotting and planning to tear it down so they could destroy the Kingdom

---

5. Psalm 2:1

it protected, and these officers were orchestrating the battle. As I heard more of their conversation, I realized this was a gathering of all the earth's prominent rulers, who were addressing the kings of the earth, outlining the next phase of their assault against this one Kingdom they utterly despised.

The malice was palpable in the voice of these kings and rulers who spoke against the Lord and His Anointed. They exhorted each other to burst apart the bonds of the Lord and His Anointed and to cast away the cords binding them to the nations. The setting and scene appeared to be ancient, but this ethos of lawlessness and its seething hatred of all things righteous seemed scarily familiar to me. I have heard of these vain murmurings happening in the halls of lawmakers, in the mansions of presidents, and in the palaces of kings. I will have nothing to do with this nonsense, and neither will my King, for He who sits in the heavens laughs; our Lord and King holds them in derision. Though they hatch their plots to conquer this Kingdom and our King, sitting atop the holy hill called Zion, their failure is already recorded and is as if written in the stars I see above.

I hear the uplifted voices of the angelic choir, and their song drowns out the noise of battle as I focus on the words. They tell the story of our Lord's only begotten Son and how the Father will make the nations His heritage and the ends of the earth His possession. Though I am focused on hearing the song, I suddenly see a disturbance on the horizon of the battlefield . . . and then I see the King's Son! The title, "King of kings and Lord of lords" is befitting to the One who leads every Believer through the gates into this Kingdom. He is magnificent beyond belief, and His enemies quake with terror as He strides through the sons of lawlessness, striking down all the outside kingdoms who refuse to turn to the King for refuge.

Having gleaned the essence of the spiritual message I am to take away from this room, I remove the glasses covering my eyes.

The King's 19th Palace

The quality of the virtual-reality effect they produce is incomparable, even set against the best high-definition gaming glasses I have previously experienced. I had, after all, been frozen in terror when they instantly translated me into the midst of the battle. Now, as I removed them, I found myself back in the room at the edge of the desk, looking past the balcony at the battle below, still raging beyond the wall.

I'm excited beyond measure, thrilled at what I witnessed in this up-close-and-personal interaction, and quite keen to keep searching this mystical landscape, this divine architectural masterpiece! How do I even begin to describe it? Thus far it seems to be a system of caves redolent with fluctuating significance, expressed as buildings or books, rooms or chapters, and depicting Bible verses through songs that portray holographic history.

I place the glasses on the table and find myself thinking about the next room I will visit. But before I start looking for the next inscription, I pause to rest and take the time to immerse myself in the marvel and beauty of what I have just experienced. I make a point of infusing into my spirit the essence of the message I received in this room:

> Whatever our position or status, serve the awesome and almighty Lord with fear, and embrace the Son so you will not perish, for blessed are all who take refuge in Him.

Mulling over this simple recall of my experience in this room, a summary of the second psalm, I consider a few prominent global leaders, and I wonder if they are supporting the Father's will in shaping their nations to become part of His Son's heritage. I consider the administration currently in power in my own nation, and I'm not convinced we're on the right track. Also, how do I apply what I have experienced to myself—to my every thought, word, and deed?

I say a prayer for my nation and its leaders, asking the Father to bring their hearts into alignment with His Word. I rise now and step through the oval doorway that stretched out from the smaller portal. I'm pleased to see this doorway has remained open while I explored the room, unlike the doorway in the wall of the high-domed crystal cavern leading to the cavern of light, which seems to close once I step through it. I am back on the stone bench in the cavern of light, and as I turn around to put my palms to the wall, I see the doorway I just exited has retreated into a small portal again. I run my hand around the edge of the portal, and when I reach full circle, the portal closes, leaving only the glowing inscription that slowly fades away.

I place my palms on the wall, and not even a foot to the left, another inscription starts pulsing with light. I place my palm over the inscription, and the choir starts singing the signature theme of this room: "O Lord, how many are my foes! Many are rising against me . . . ." I recognize the song as a psalm of David, and with this realization I make the connection that it follows on from the previous psalm I just finished exploring. It seems the Master Architect is guiding me through the book of Psalms in a consecutive manner. I decide to enter the room, and the portal widens immediately into an oval doorway that I step through.

The room I am in is small, and the wall in front of me has glowing Hebrew characters inscribed, about head high. The inscription widens immediately into an oval doorway when I place my palm on it, and I step through into another small room. This room resembles the previous one, and as I hear the words underpinning this room in song, I realize it, too, has a glowing inscription on the wall. I repeat the process of opening the doorway, and when I step into the third room, I realize these three rooms are interconnected. Even so,

The King's 19th Palace

I have a sense they are distinctly separate, so I go back to the first room, where the singing of this psalm of David again greets my ears. I make a mental note about the layout of these three rooms which, by their words, I realize are mirroring the third, fourth, and fifth psalms.

Immediately a feeling comes over me. I'm filled with confidence, knowing I can face both today and tomorrow, no matter the problem or foe I may encounter. It feels good to be in the house of the Lord! These rooms have a theme in common and bring to mind several thoughts that are manifested in front of me like holograms. I see myself throughout every day being faced with some adversary, whether in the form of a person or a situation, and fully realize my King is an encompassing shield about me, and He is also the lifter and sustainer of my head. The King not only answers me throughout the day but also when I lie down to sleep. When I wake, the King will be there yet again, supporting me entirely. I see myself walking between the three rooms, noticing small differences as well as constant changes in the layout and furnishings, yet in each of the rooms I am given a sense of my King's awe-inspiring power. I feel energized, and I have no reason to be afraid, for what can any man do to me? My King answers me; He gives me relief in distress and is leading me in His ways, each and every step I take.

The atmosphere in these rooms—and the songs reflecting the words that create the rooms—lead me to think of children's nighttime poems. I have several songs swirling in my head based on these words, including "Because He lives, I can face tomorrow. Because He lives, all fear is gone." I specifically walk back into each of the three rooms again to lift my voice in praise, and as I do, the choir is suddenly muted. I can still hear the whisper of each room's theme song when I stop singing, but as soon as I raise my own voice, the choir is automatically muted again. I go to the first of the three rooms, and I sing a heartfelt rendition of "You are a shield about me, the lifter of my head." I then move to the second room, and in here I sing the children's poem, "When I lie down to sleep, I pray and know my soul my King will safely keep." I reach the third room and lift my voice in song, first singing, "When Morning Gilds the Skies" followed by "My Faith Looks Up to You."

I step through the oval doorway into the chamber of light, and I close the portal behind me. I stay silent for a moment, absorbing the beauty and capturing my thoughts summarizing the three rooms I just visited: Despite the number of foes rising against me, my King is a shield about me, protecting and sustaining me. Righteous anger has its place, but I must not sin! Because I take refuge in my King, I can freely rejoice, knowing He spreads His protection over me, blessing me and covering me with His favor as with a shield.

It's too easy to lose track of time when I'm having so much fun, so I call it a day. Now, however, I am faced with the task of finding my way back to the crystal cave. On both occasions my entrance into the cave of light was from the wall opposite the stone bench, so I step down onto the floor and walk across the room to where I expect the doorway to be. I see no sign of a crystal to twist, so I try using the second method of intercave travel I have learned. Starting at the corner of the room, my palms against the wall, I start moving to my left. About ten yards along, I feel a familiar heat emanating from the wall, so I stop and wait. Sure enough, I see an inscription forming. I place my flat palm over the characters, and a portal opens in the wall. I found it! I'm looking into the crystal cave. I make my way back to the cave adjacent to the overhang, and leaving my knapsack near the circle of stones where I made my fire, I head out for a swim in the river.

Ephesians 6 is a "room" teaching us about the full armor of God our King—the armor He provides for each of us as soldiers in His mighty army. Note that all the armor is protective except for one item, the Sword

of the Spirit, which is the truth of His Word He equips us with to fight against the words of the enemy. Also note, there is no armor protecting our backs. We are to always face the battle with His truth, knowing our Lord is not only the Leader of the battle but also has our back!

Chapter 5

Who can ascend to the King's holy hill or dwell with Him there? Only those with clean hands, a pure heart, and blameless walk, who speak truth and do what is right. Only by His change in me can I go! (based on Psalm 15:1–2 and 24:3–4).

I sleep soundly in this cave. I wake feeling refreshed and excited to face the day. I go through my usual morning routine: I start a fire, take a quick swim in the river to freshen up, brew some coffee, and make a simple breakfast. I'm keen to explore the next room or set of rooms—I've now realized some rooms have a common theme threaded through interconnecting doors. I pour some sand onto my fire, fill my water bottle, and set off to the crystal cave. I turn the amethyst to gain entrance to the chamber of light, step up onto the bench across the room, and I start exploring the next section of wall.

I find the next "key" to room 6 a few inches farther along the wall from where I was given access to room 5. I place my palm over the glowing inscription until the portal stretches out into an oval doorway. The room doesn't initially seem any different than the previous rooms I visited, but as I enter this room, I experience dread and fear . . . unlike the other rooms, the song I hear is being sung in a low bass tone. It also has a dirgelike quality to it, as though a lament or song of sorrow. I recognize it as a psalm of David, whose very bones and soul are greatly troubled as he languishes in a pit of despair. I feel restless as I take a few cautious steps, moving deeper into the room. As I approach a sturdy couch covered with an exotic pattern of weaved cloth, I lie down and realize the cloth is wet to my touch. At that moment the words of a bleak song break through into my conscious mind: "I am weary with my moaning; every night I flood my bed with tears; I drench my couch with my weeping. My eye wastes away because of grief . . ."

These are somber images that leave me contemplating the vast array of ills afflicting so many billions of people in my contemporary world.

But then the tempo changes, switching to a driving, upbeat rhythm. There is no trace of the dread and fear I first felt, and the voices have switched to a tenor. The higher notes also have a lighter, more positive expression, and this is mirrored by the comforting words I now hear, confirming the Lord has heard my plea and accepts my prayer. My enemies shall turn back and be put to shame in a moment. My King relieves and delivers. I can approach the King freely when I am afraid or fearful and trust in His unfailing care and deliverance. I can sing, "When I am afraid, I will trust in Him."

Feeling at peace now, I open my eyes to see a wall with no hanging pictures or furniture blocking it. I anticipate there might be another room behind the wall. As I touch the wall, a small room like a secret closet opens—directly connected to room 6—I have an overwhelming sensation, knowing at all times and in every circumstance I can safely take refuge in the King, for He is a righteous judge . . . not only of me but also my adversaries. I lift my voice in song, singing an appropriate song: "You Are My Hiding Place."

I walk only a couple steps and find the back wall of the closet free of obstruction and find myself quickly in room 8. I immediately see heavens with their numerous distant stars and something like arms or hands moving stars as I hear the faint echo of pulsars and infants joining in a receding song I recognize. I can't help raising my voice to join in a soft and meaningful rendition. I start out singing, "O Lord our Lord, how majestic is Your name in all the earth!" Only when my song ends does an angelic choir then repeat the words, reminding me *who* created this room, and I drink in my smallness and the magnificence of my Creator. I stand gazing as I marvel at the word "majestic," which informs us the King is both powerful *and* He is our Lord—He is Creator of everything magnificent, glorious, and beautiful. I am a mere man created by Him *and* in His image—He has crowned me with a portion of that glory and majesty. Just as He cares for me, He also gives me charge to care for a portion of His creation. How majestic is the name of our God, who sets His glory above the heavens!

I open the next portal and enter into still another room that is clearly labeled 9. Looking around I see telltale signs of a dividing wall erected in this room. The bricks in this wall are different to the other three walls, so I approach the wall, and indeed, I can open a doorway into still another room. I remember a piece of information I hadn't paid much attention to, but it sparks my memory as I now see the physical proof of it. Some authorities uncovered evidence these two rooms were originally one, before being moved to become a part of this palace. I give thanks to the King for all of the wonderful things He has done—I was reminded of His accomplishments in room 8, and now I am visiting a fortress converted to a museum, amazed at the ancient bronze military items scattered throughout these connected rooms, 9 and 10. I notice and then pick up a bronze helmet so heavy I can barely lift it. I put it over my head, but it dwarfs me—it must have belonged to a giant!

I place the helmet back in its cabinet then turn to admire a bronze coat of chain mail that covers most of one wall. I have always been intrigued by the enormity of Old Testament giants, and now I stand witness—I presume these ancient relics I see are the war spoils of the shepherd boy, David, on the day he defeated Goliath. After all, who else carried a spear whose shaft was like a weaver's beam? I marvel at this huge, rounded wooden beam, and then I see just the head of the spear, detached, displayed on a shelf. I estimate its weight to be about 30 pounds. The choir sings the words that account the creation of these rooms, and the words blend seamlessly as I cross the threshold between the two rooms once more. They sing about how the nations sunk into the pit they made, and how—in the net that they hid from enemies—their own foot was caught. I know these words relate to the Philistines and how all the wicked nations surrounding Israel often were caught in their own schemes, but I also recognize the timeless beauty of the King's message, which is more relevant today than ever before.

I am reminded of my experience in room 2 with the virtual-reality glasses, where I bore witness to the raging of the nations and how the people were plotting in vain . . . and how today's prominent global leaders are not supporting the Father's will in shaping their nations to become part of His Son's heritage. I can only pray the Lord makes Himself known and executes judgment today as He did on the ancient battlefield that gave rise to this marvelous edifice and museum. Maybe the day has finally come for the wicked to be snared in the work of their own hands. He is the awesome King who reigns in majesty. I feel His presence in this place, and I thank Him for His correct judgment and perfect justice, always provided at exactly the right time. We are human and have imperfect lives and make imperfect judgments, but we can put our trust completely in our King and in His perfect timing.

Seeing no apparent options for further advancement beyond room 10, I make my way back to the chamber of light. I walk along the stone bench with outstretched palms until I find the next inscription key. I open the doorway to room 11 and start exploring. I'm taking notes as I go because I must share this experience with whoever has ears to hear. I love the entranceway of this room, and

Dr. Gene Baillie

I stand admiring this peaceful and secure cathedral-like room from this vantage point for a moment. The choir is singing with gusto, and their first refrain reminds me I've taken refuge in my Lord, who ensures my security. I pass a small alcove where, placed on an ornate wooden side table, I see a pair of glasses. I put on the virtual-reality glasses, and immediately I realize I am a bird flying through a window outside the room and above wicked men shooting arrows zinging close by. An uncomfortable wave of dread envelopes me as I now hear words speaking of the King knowing and seeing me completely. I see buildings crumbling into piles of rubble, collapsing because of stress in their foundations, cracking and splintering apart from the bottom upward. Is my foundation really secure? I realize I am being tested—what can I do?

Most times we want to quickly turn tail and run away when we see that first arrow coming our way. As I see these ancient structures crumbling and being destroyed right down to their foundations, I would join them in saying, "What can even a righteous person do?" Yet we have an excellent reason not to flee, knowing our King is on the throne. He sees what the wicked are doing as He tests them, but He is also testing us, the righteous. I want to have His face gaze on me as I find my refuge in Him. I want a firm foundation. I need to completely depend on Him, *in Him*, and *for Him*, absolutely everything! He directs my steps and keeps me on the right path, the narrow path, along which we—as the King's children—stride purposefully, joined by countless others whose hearts now also follow Him. I return the glasses to the ornate wooden side table, and I leave the room.

The next glowing inscription is farther along the stone bench than I expected, but the portal and doorway open in the usual manner. Because the Psalms are a collection of songs of praise to the King, I have become accustomed to hearing angelic voices singing familiar words or teachings when I enter a room. But as I look around, I feel quite alone. I then hear whispers of a song that speaks of how the faithful have vanished from among the children of man. I put on the virtual-reality glasses as I listen to the words of the song, recognizing that people through the ages have uttered lies to their neighbors with flattering lips and how they speak with a double heart. I recognize my own predisposition—an innate tendency, perhaps—to want to be liked, to say the right things, and to be considered important. I also have times when I flatter and stretch the truth in deception, if not actually lie. I too suffer from being double-minded.

There is, however, a contrast between my human speech and those words I now hear the King speaking—I notice a vessel of silver upon a hot fire with a metal ladle repeatedly removing dross from the top—the King's words are clean and pure like this silver refined *seven times,* meaning absolutely all the dross or impurity is absent. As I turn, I hear the final refrain the angelic choir sings, woven like silver strands into the very fabric creating the walls of this room. I am that fabric! They sing about how, even though on every side the wicked prowl and vileness is exalted among the children of man, our King will keep and guard us from my generation onward forever. As I lower the glasses, I ponder the meaning of the number 7—knowing it represents completeness or perfection.

I move along the bench and enter room 13. As I cross the threshold into this room, I lift my glasses and am struck by a recurring theme evident in several of the rooms I recently visited. For my benefit—and yours—the King has provided this repeating theme of waiting on and for Him. I hear it again now: "How long, O Lord?" As I listen to the words, they are literally upholding this structure and room, and I realize this repetition is to impress upon me and remind me repeatedly I am to wait on my Lord, and to trust this One who upholds me completely. I have a sense it is to keep me mindful of my salvation, and to keep me cognizant of how the Lord has dealt bountifully with me. His ways are far superior to ours—unlike the uncertainty we display in our human insecurity, not like the person I see now pulling petals from a rose, saying, "He loves me, He loves me not," but rather, "He loves me always and completely! Then appears His cup of love, always full and overflowing." As I somehow now experience love overflowing, I really cannot explain in words. I leave this room singing a special song that comes to mind from another palace in our King's Kingdom, Lamentations 3:22–23: "The steadfast love of the Lord never ceases, His mercies never come to an end.; they are new every morning, great is your faithfulness."

Room 14 brings to mind sadness as I hear out of darkness and then see those who are fools with their foolish words parading proudly before me. But then I perceive also the wonder of this Kingdom I am exploring. While I am currently touring through this awe-inspiring palace of my King, I remember it is but one of 66 buildings this great Architect and Builder has constructed. I am in a room that is completely dark as the choir sings, and except for minor changes, I will later find the same basic construction plan and furnishings in room 53. I know, too, some of these important items are also repeated within the third room in the Romans house, items 9 to 18. The word "fool" in the context of this room is not to imply someone who is ignorant, but rather a person who is foolish in the sense of not apprehending the obvious knowledge and truth about the King and who He is. Without acting on the King's prompting, and His encouragement for us to embrace His truth, *we are all such fools*. I witness as I see them not only turn but actually walk away from the King. (I perceive that since such a person does not have the ability to know or even see the King in any sense, instead they walk in a direction of their own choosing, which is *always* the wrong direction.) It is impossible for such a fool to do anything good. Our hope lies in the salvation that will come out of our King's highest hill called Zion!

As I leave the 14th room and now enter the 15th, it is like leaving the darkness of night and walking into the brightness of the

The King's 19th Palace

noonday sun. I lift my glasses and feel joy in the reality of seeing myself standing in this glorious light. Lowering the glasses, I have a vibrant new heart, hearing it speak truth back to me, and am seeking after another heart, high and lifted up. I am so thankful my Lord has not only changed me and put me on the right path I am now walking, but also, I see a house He has provided as a dwelling place for me—now and forever. I am immediately drawn to the specific signpost pointing to the King's house as our place to sojourn, dwell, or rest. *How am I even allowed to enter this room, let alone any room in any house of the King?* I wonder. Then I remember and see I have been given an admission jacket. I am an adopted child entering his father's dwelling; I am only able to do this because of that jacket of perfection, righteousness, and truth He (the King, my Father) has given me. I cannot enter on my own merit or ability but, rather, because the King has changed my heart and my very being. Otherwise, I would still be the fool described in the previous room. As I hear the choir sing the last verse of the words that uphold this room, I visualize myself as I join a marching throng, and we sing, "Marching to Zion." Glorious Zion, the King's residence on His holy hill.

When I return to the chamber of light, I am keen to continue my exploration of this exquisitely crafted 19th Palace of my King, but I feel physically weary. The timelessness within the palace and the powerful emotions these "rooms-wrought-from-song" elicit within me leave my body spent but my spirit replete with well-being. At the end of each day's exploration, I leave filled with peace and an indescribable inner joy. I'm never sure what time of my earthly day I will return to when I squeeze through the tunnel leading from the first cave to the overhang outside. I glance at my watch, but somehow there is nothing apparent on the dial! This seems to confirm that space and time meld into one spiritual truth that defies physical reality or even time at all in this place, just as I saw my hand meld with the walls of stone built upon the central Cornerstone, our everlasting Rock. I want to call it a day, but my curiosity gets the better of me, so I decide to have a look at the 16th room. This room holds great significance for me, and I want a glimpse inside before I leave these subterranean caverns of mystery and delight. I want to hold the image in my mind, so I can meditate on it after dinner, gazing into the fire.

So on the wall to the left of where room 15 appeared, I take only two steps to the left and again feel that strange heat emanating from the wall—it never ceases to amaze me—as between my hands I see an inscription becoming visible. I hold my hands steady as the characters complete their form. The Hebrew symbols shimmer with radiant light, and I remove my palms from the wall. I scrutinize the symbols closely, and although I am not versed in Hebrew numbers, I feel certain they represent the number 16: ט״ז

Feeling strangely nervous and excited, I place the palm of my right hand over the newly formed symbols. I have grown to cherish the sensation of my hand melding with the wall as I touch the inscription and my arm vibrates gently. The portal opens, and the sound of those heavenly voices rises in song: "Preserve me, O God, for in you I take refuge." I gaze longingly into this special room, drinking in the richness of the tapestries cladding the walls, the heavy, hardwood furniture, and the bright, shimmering sheen the room projects. I stand in awe, lost in the moment. I am tempted to place my palm over the portal to open the doorway, but I relent. I've had my sneak peek. I will have the strength and vigor to explore this special chamber on another visit, and with my glasses. I brush my open palm across the portal, and it slowly closes from the outer edges toward the middle. The image of the room is emblazoned upon my mind, as if it were the shutter of a camera lens closing, leaving me with this imprinted snapshot I will cherish.

When I reach the overhang, I glance at my watch again, seeing the time clearly now, and outside there is still some daylight left as I make my way down to the river. I sing a song of praise to my King while I collect firewood, feeling refreshed after my swim. Later, I gaze into the fire, lost in reverie. I hold the image of rich tapestries and solid furniture in my mind, and it becomes superimposed onto my fire, as it changes into a vibrant and mesmerizing display of dancing color and light that only a campfire can do. I sleep soundly in this cave. Tonight my dreams are filled with a sense of safety, security, joy, and eternal pleasure.

Chapter 6

After this I looked, and behold, a door standing open in heaven! And the first voice, which I had heard speaking to me like a trumpet, said, "Come up here, and I will show you what must take place after this." At once I was in the Spirit, and behold, a throne stood in heaven, with one seated on the throne. Revelation 4:1–2

I really wanted to spend more time in room 15. In fact, I wanted to take up residence in room 15, especially because I felt like such a favored and welcome guest in its environment. I truly knew I was and always would be an adopted son of the King while listening to the words of the song about dwelling with Him in His Kingdom. I wanted to continue marching with the gathering throng. I also knew this room to be a special tent of my Father, and my mind was filled with the beauty of its construction as I lay between sleep and waking on the morning after my visit. I replayed the entire scene in my mind, then feeling blessed and relaxed, I ran through the sequence of events that led me to peek into room 16.

I was sorely tempted to spend another day exploring the many rooms within the 19th Palace of the King, but I had family commitments. Some months back we had booked a trip to Kartchner Caverns State Park in Arizona, and while I had eagerly anticipated this family excursion, I was frustrated knowing I would have to put room 16 on hold for a time. I rose from my sleeping bag, and after a quick swim, I packed my backpack and set out along the path to my truck. The five-mile hike had me perspiring, and it was great to be inside my air-conditioned vehicle. My drive home was uneventful, and I arrived in time for a delicious lunch prepared by my wife, Carol. My daughter, Mary, and her husband, Eric, would be joining us on our Arizona caving trip, as well as their children, John and Elizabeth. They had all arrived shortly before I did, and the excitement grew as we discussed our imminent journey.

After an early dinner, I regaled my family with the wonders I had perceived in the caves beneath the Appalachian foothills, and I told them how excited I was to soon return. We sang a few of the hymns connected to the King's 19th Palace before turning in, knowing we had an early start to catch our "dark:30" morning flight to Tucson.

During the rental car drive from the Tucson airport, my daughter read some background info to us while we drove to Kartchner Caverns, first discovered in 1974 by two friends who were exploring the limestone hills at the eastern base of the Whetstone Mountains. Southern Arizona has a unique and tranquil beauty, with a variety of birds and wildlife in the desert backcountry. Mary was keen to capture some images with a new camera Eric recently gave her for her birthday.

After our early arrival at the state park, we were directed to a two-room, air-conditioned camping cabin with a view of the Whetstone Mountains. We had booked the following day to explore Kartchner Caverns, so we decided to spend the day on an ambitious tour, visiting first the natural riparian area of the Murray Springs Clovis Site. Its archaeology contains an undisturbed stratigraphic record of the past 40,000 years, including the nearby woolly mammoth bones located in one of the oldest native American hunting sites in North America. Then on we went to Whitewater Draw with an incredible number of migrating Sandhill cranes, which reminded me of my childhood days seeing more than 100,000 of these special birds nesting and foraging along the Platte River in central Nebraska. We had just enough time to drive back through Bisbee, Lowell, and Tombstone to take in the old Wild West and ghost towns with copper and silver mining history as well. It was a fun-filled afternoon, and we arrived back at the cabin before sunset, in time to grill supper outside and enjoy quality time together around the fire.

We rose early the following morning, leaving our daypacks in the lockers, so we could easily access our snacks and drinks once our tour was complete. Our guide led the way down into the cave, and we followed, along with another family of three. We had booked the Throne Room Tour, which takes just under two hours to complete. We began our exploration walking in single file, and our guide occasionally halted the group to discuss the intricate details of the limestone rock formations. Limestone is soluble in water, so when water interacts with it, the rock dissolves, and the water carries away some of the minerals. These minerals also contribute to the formation of stalactites, stalagmites, and helictites, the latter resembling soda-straw-like tubes created by individual drops of water depositing calcium carbonate around the rim. Instead of always ascending and descending vertically—as do stalactites and stalagmites—some helictites also extend almost horizontally or diagonally and can display a curving or angular form that looks as if they have grown in zero gravity, which is simply amazing and something I knew nothing about.

About a half hour into the tour, I was distracted by a sharply-faceted stone protruding from a wall just beyond the pathway. I was at the back of the group when I glanced up to see it was an amethyst, much like the crystal that had given me entrance into the chamber of light beneath the Appalachian foothills. My heart began hammering in my chest . . . could this be another opening into the King's 19th Palace?

The King's 19th Palace

    I desperately wanted to touch the amethyst, feeling almost certain that if I reached out my hand and applied pressure with my thumb and forefinger, I could expect to hear the grating noise as the rock opened before me. I had to restrain myself, though, as visitors are forbidden to touch anything underground. The oil from our fingers will hinder the growth of the mineral structures, so I felt duty-bound to protect the magnificent limestone formations beyond our visit, as they only grow about an inch over a 100-year period. While I stood before the amethyst, I heard approaching voices—my entire family had come back to look for me. I took a step back toward the path, and as I did, I saw an inscription forming on the bedrock at my feet. I stood in awe as the Hebrew symbols began pulsing, emitting a soft, radiant glow.

    Struck with a sudden intuitive sense, I reached my hand out to my granddaughter, Elizabeth. She took my hand, and before anyone could utter a word, I told the rest of my family to join hands. They were all so used to me praying that, despite the strange circumstance we were in, my family quickly followed my suggestion, looking at me to start my prayer. They were no doubt wondering what specific wonder had inspired me to offer up a prayer of thanksgiving. Without saying another word, I placed my right foot over the glowing Hebrew inscription.

    Although half expecting to hear the grating sound, what happened next was quite unexpected. We all experienced vertigo and loss of orientation, similar to the sensation I first experienced when entering the chamber of light. We discussed it later that evening, and during our transition between the Throne Room Tour and the entryway to the King's 19th Palace, we all recounted experiencing a kaleidoscope of light and color shimmering across the cave walls like a strobe light. When the sensation passed, we were in a completely different setting. Despite having experienced this strange room change in the Appalachian foothills, it was the last thing I expected here in southern Arizona. Once my eyes had adjusted to the soft glow of our new surroundings, I was awe-stricken. We were standing in a giant thronelike cavern formed long ago by water seeping through the limestone and dissolving it, forming these magnificent sheets, drapes, chandeliers, and soda-straw structures, similar to what we had seen on the other side of this "doorway"—but on a much grander scale. I noticed a huge rock and arch that was exactly like the cornerstone/capstone combination I had seen in the Carolinas, but atop was a massive chairlike structure like a throne.

"Dad . . . what's happening?"

"Welcome to the King's 19th Palace, Mary." My daughter stared at me, unable to argue the point but struggling to grasp what had just happened. I put a hand on her shoulder. "This is what I was describing to all of you last night. These doorways into this different reality are obviously not just confined to the Appalachian foothills."

"Wow! This is so cool!" John was turning in a slow circle, taking in the magnificence of our surroundings. Elizabeth, who was still holding Mary's hand, looked slightly concerned.

"Don't worry," I spoke softly to her. "Whatever mystery we are experiencing, our heavenly Father is orchestrating it for your and all our benefit. We have nothing to fear." Elizabeth released her mother's hand and smiled at me, looking more confident at my assurance we were safe. Eric and John were already a few paces away, exploring our new environment while whistling and high-fiving each other like a pair of schoolboys.

I turned slowly, in a 360-degree circle, seeing a number of interesting rock formations. There were sidewise helictites but huge and at steep angles. In some areas there were stalagmites, stalactites, and even columns that had variable content comprising their structure—shiny specks of crystallite making up the base and extending to a certain height then suddenly transitioning to a different color and mineral content within the space of a few inches. It was truly awe-inspiring.

The King's 19th Palace

I approached a tall, thick column, tempted to reach out and feel the texture of a color transition, wondering if it would vary in texture as the color changed. I fought this temptation, choosing rather to study the formation up close. There seemed to be no discernible difference in texture, but as I drew back from the rock, I suddenly felt a strange heat emanating from the wall. Besides the emotions this heat elicited—which seemed dreamlike or even spiritual within my being—I also felt an internal, biochemical tripswitch rapidly increase the pace of my beating heart as I saw an inscription becoming visible in the rock before my eyes. I watched the symbols develop, as though I were watching a print develop in a darkroom, except the image was holographic, hovering a few inches above the rock formation.

How can this be? Is it possible this could be yet another doorway leading into the King's 19th Palace? It struck me this room was probably an anteroom where we could choose to enter different rooms of the palace, much like in the chamber of light where I could stand on the stone bench to access other numerous rooms of the King's palace. I looked closely at the symbol—it was a replica of the last Hebrew number I had seen while standing on the stone bench in the chamber of light—it was the Hebrew number 16: עייד. I took a deep breath then stepped nearer the newly formed holographic symbol. My arm immediately began to vibrate, and I experienced that exhilarating sensation of my feet melding with the stone floor. I raised my left hand and summoned my family as a doorway appeared.

The doorway to the room opened of its own volition, and I heard the sound of angelic voices rising in song: "Preserve me, O God, for in you I take refuge." I was so excited I did a little mental happy dance, fascinated at the depth of reach my King had into our natural world. This was the *exact* room I witnessed just two days' prior—it had the same rich tapestries cladding the walls, the same heavy, hardwood furniture, and the room projected the same bright, shimmering sheen I had glimpsed in the caves beneath the Appalachian foothills.

As I began exploring room 16, my family quickly gathered around me, and I could see the reverence on their faces as we stared into the room. It was like looking at the imprinted snapshot that had been emblazoned upon my mind, but this time I did not hesitate—I stepped boldly across the threshold into the room. I was followed by Carol then the others, and as we entered, there was a palpable Presence. We all felt the safety and security our Father the King always provides for us, especially when we enter into His presence through His Word.

I always feel His protection, irrespective of where I am within the space-time continuum of our universe. To my left I see an exquisite olivewood table, and on the polished surface I see a symbol I have grown to recognize in the King's palace—a pair of glasses, arms invitingly open and a tool to benefit my deeper insight. I pick up the glasses and hand them to Carol, but as she places them on the bridge of her nose, another pair appears on the olivewood table. I hand them to Mary, and the process is repeated, with another pair becoming immediately available. Finally, we are all wearing these special glasses, and our perspective broadens to see ourselves included with all the saints within a biblical landscape—they are the excellent ones, our brethren in whom we delight. We can all see each other, and together we realize our King is doing everything for our good. We also realize the King is apportioning a fenced-out area to all the saints within His Kingdom, and each of us is included.

As I realize I am in my assigned place, I note my measured-out portion includes so much more than I could ever have expected. Because I know the Lord is my portion and my cup, He has preserved and kept my lot, safe from the ravages of rust and moth and thief. It is really a pleasant "lot" in so many wonderful ways. The fence lines have fallen for me in pleasant places; indeed, I have a beautiful inheritance. I am in awe of everything, knowing I have already been given this lot to inhabit every day of my life. It thrills me to know my grandchildren, John and Elizabeth, are also nearby on this side of this portal. I can see them but wonder what they are perceiving. I want them to receive not only this visible but also all the invisible portion I am recognizing. Thus I am inspired to do my part to further instill the wisdom of our King into their young souls, passing on the legacy of faith I have been given. My heart is pulled toward these precious children, and although my carnal mind tries to caution me this adventure may be dangerous for them, I am aware of the King's presence within this experience, so I refuse to fret, knowing my family will ultimately be safe within this Kingdom.

Filled with gratitude at being given the "key" to this awe-inspiring landscape, at the far end of the room, I see words on the wall. They all start with "p," and I realize I have experienced every one: pasture, place, pleasant, portion, provision, purpose, protection, presence, and preservation. When I get closer, I see smaller writing and a carefully concealed large wooden door, and carved into it at eye-level I see—surprisingly—the words are written in English: "Secret Passageway." I encountered similar "secret doors" between rooms on my previous visits to the chamber of light, so I call Carol over to explore the new passageway. We hold hands, and when I turn the door handle, it leads us directly into room 23. We hear the opening chorus of the words that create this splendid room: "The Lord is my shepherd; I shall not want. He makes me lie down in green pastures."

Our virtual-reality glasses present this room to us on our mutual journey, with its resplendent shepherd-and-sheep metaphor aspects. I have known this place since childhood, and I have spent some quality moments in this space, but each time I understand more. On this occasion, however, I see a passage leading off from a sidewall, and while Carol starts exploring items on a shelf in the far corner of the room, I follow the passage. I reach another turn that immediately opens up onto a balcony. I stand on the balcony, holding an iron railing, where I can look over the entire property of this Kingdom with all of its houses. I see the Kingdom landscape clearly from this vantage point, and I realize my pleasant lot extends to the far reaches of the property, and the edge is bordered with a strong fence. It is the same fence I had walked along on the outside so many years ago, which kept me from entering into this Kingdom illegally.

I remember considering numerous ways to gain access before meeting the King, but try as I might, I was unable to climb over the fence or skirt around it, and neither was I able to dig underneath it. I stood by the main gate of this Kingdom many times, but I soon realized it was extremely secure and guarded—there was simply no way I could gain access. Now that I know the King and His Son welcomed me into the Kingdom, I realize this fence around my portion has two purposes: to keep out all the illegal aliens and other harmful elements of the evil one—those whose only choice is *not to serve* the King—but also to define the extent of my freedom within the security of the Kingdom—a demarcated border to ensure I do not inadvertently (and really cannot) stray into the darkness beyond.

My mind wanders back to my childhood—I grew up on a farm where we kept animals, and included in the infrastructure were fences with barbed wire tightly strung to sturdy posts. The fences had this same twofold purpose: they protected the animals from straying beyond the border of the farm, but the fence also prevented other dangers from entering into our property. I remember placing (and later replacing) the fence posts along the fence line, planning carefully to avoid any obstacles. Those fence posts reminded me now of the various important junctures in my own life, as well as marking specific changes in the direction of my life.

As my mind returned to my present "lot," I also remembered walking on the outside and wondering what all the fuss was about concerning the people, structures, and promises within. I was quite curious at that time, but I simply could not see beyond the Kingdom border, feeling frustrated at not knowing what was happening within its boundaries. I had heard stories of people trying to gain access to the Kingdom using their own abilities, but they were unable to penetrate the fence. I had also heard of others who were blinded by a bright light, while some people had even heard the voice of the King or one of His servants speaking to them. I now know the King chose, directed, and provided for these experiences, enabling these people to embrace Him, and who were then accepted as adopted sons and daughters into His Kingdom.

In my past, I have to admit I was curious, and desperately wanted access to this Kingdom but for all the wrong reasons. I wanted to be in control, to study and determine for myself the best path for my own life and the way I would walk. Then one day when I was in the midst of a challenging situation, I realized I could not control my life path—and indeed, I was *not* in control. This event occurred while I was helping out in a mission hospital in Korea. One morning, one of the other doctors gave morning devotions and began his message with a quote: "A man plans his way or considers his path, but the Lord guides and directs each step he takes or the specific way he goes." That is my own translation of this important writing I have studied in the King's Palace of Proverbs. Bingo! I realized I was not in control and immediately sought out this Lord who could direct my steps. That very day the King's Son led me right up to the gate; it was opened, and I was given the right to dwell in this pleasant lot—and I have been dwelling here happily, ever since.

Although that last sentence may sound rather glib and matter of fact, the details reveal my deeper concerns—I did not know much at all about this Kingdom, nor what to expect once I was allowed entry. I had heard about the King who ruled and lived here. I had also heard He had servants, whom some even called slaves. Was this a prison? Once I was permitted into the Kingdom, I was told my life would now be heading in a completely opposite direction. It was all very confusing! I heard the King was holy and would judge me. I was told I would come to understand the good news, which was, simply put, the King's Son had taken my place in every way, every trial, and every circumstance. His obedience would replace my disobedience; He would be judged for my sins. Not the message I thought I would hear, but soon I learned the difference in our usual thoughts of a slave and realized it meant a willing servant and follower.

Thus, I found I would dwell within His Kingdom inside this gate as an adopted son. I became obedient, though not perfectly. I endeavored to please the King, realizing I wanted to serve Him in whatever manner He directed me. *He* was now in control, *not* me. I began to increasingly understand His holiness, grace, love, and mercy—things I now desire to be expressed in my every thought, word, and deed. I became a willful servant, able to please and praise. I had been sitting in darkness and was suddenly brought into the all-revealing Light—I was changed completely, finally able to see. I now truly understood the song I had heard sung around a campfire so many years ago, a song I still sing quite often: "Amazing Grace." I once was blind but now I see. Way beyond physical sight and perception. And now I realize He chose me and gave me the ability to respond!

I have everything I need. He cares for me like a shepherd cares for his flock of sheep, paying close attention, even to the small and the weak. He makes sure I have the best food and water and keeps me safe. He gives me new strength and helps me to do what honors Him most. Even when I am close to death, I am not afraid; I feel He is close, protecting me. He feeds me well despite my circumstances and honors me as a guest; He gives me so much my cup overflows. My Shepherd's kindness and love are always with me, and I will love Him forever.

I left the balcony, returning to the main part of room 23 with continuing thoughts of my Shepherd, Savior, King, and Guide. Carol must have called the rest of the family because they were all in this room off the secret passageway, each one engrossed in different details around the room. I sat quietly and thanked the Lord for giving me His wise counsel and instruction, and for being with me continuously. While I have life and breath on this earth within this Kingdom, I will reside securely in His perfect, loving, and protective care. I thank Him for helping me to recognize and accept the true path to life eternal, the certain hope of dwelling with my Father forever. He is holding my hand as He guides and directs each of my steps. I motioned to my family, and we all gathered together again. I opened the wooden door, and we exited the room, going back into room 16.

I took off the glasses—I will tell you more later, about that day of sudden change that occurred within me, the day my heart was replaced. I will also tell you more about how I came to know the King had other purposes for me beyond the fence. I certainly do dwell securely within the Kingdom, but I have also been given assignments outside, beyond the Kingdom boundary.

We continued spending some time marveling at the rich tapestries that hang from the walls, the hardwood furniture, and the translucent light shimmering in a manner similar to that of the chamber of light. I had expected to spend more time here, but the secret passageway I found instead provided me with an unexpected trove of memorabilia I will forever treasure, and will be able to savor far into the future. I am overjoyed a part of my family has now been personally immersed in the beauty of this Kingdom beyond my dialog. Besides, I learned something unique today by following the path opened to me (now us)—these rooms are accessible to Kingdom people no matter where they may be on the earth. I realize wherever I may be on this planet, the Kingdom and the Word on which it is founded is always easily accessible, especially because I have His Light and eyes to see through the veil separating the physical from the spiritual and because I have been given ears to hear the words the King speaks.

Dr. Gene Baillie

We exited the portal from room 16, going back into the massive cavern that to us served a similar function to the chamber of light—it is another index room, where people can choose which room of the 19th Palace they might enter. I closed the portal behind me, and we headed back to our point of entry. I found the exact place I had been standing when the strobe lights disappeared from the cave walls. I suggested to my family we all hold hands again, and while I was still marveling at the magnificent limestone formations around us, I had the sudden sensation I was dematerializing. I felt my body becoming weightless, and instead of seeing the flesh on my body, I became aware of it emitting a radiant light. It was an unexplainable sensation, and when it passed, we were all standing just off the main path in front of the amethyst crystal I had been tempted to touch. We were back in the cavern where we were being guided through the Throne Room Tour.

I led the way now, and just around the corner, we reached the rest of our tour group. Fully aware of how time in the King's 19th Palace is often different to my everyday experience of it, I was wondering how long it had been since we last were with our group. I quickly reached the conclusion we had not even been missed because the tour guide simply smiled at me and continued chatting casually to a member of the other family touring with us. Carol caught my eye and squeezed my hand, and we shared a glance that expressed all the pent-up excitement generated by our "few seconds" of family secret adventure. As the guide pointed out the large throne with its surrounding rotunda and limestone "tapestries," my son-in-law Eric quietly noted to us it was atop a massive, seemingly perfect cube of stone!

We often speak of treasure and usually default to the idea of money. There are, however, many other instances related to the concept of

"treasuring"—especially in the sense of important or valuable concepts and teachings to remember. Later we realize how the repetition of important teachings and principles have affected every part of our lives and the way we live—each and every day. And then we learn to be truly thankful for these often indescribable treasures. We especially need to be grateful for the treasured gift of salvation granted by our Lord's sacrificial gift.

Chapter 7

*In this very room . . . I feel His presence. Because He lives,
I can face tomorrow, every fear is gone. My King wins
every battle (based on the rooms of this chapter).*

I flipped through my calendar, looking to see where I could carve out a few days to revisit the caving system in the Appalachian foothills. Carol and Mary both expressed great interest in joining me on my next expedition to the North Carolina cave, and although Eric was also keen, his work obligations prevented him from taking more time off. Besides, someone had to keep an eye on "schoolbound" Elizabeth and John. Various members of our family have planned a number of trips to foreign lands through the next six months. Our first booking is to visit the Qumran caves in Israel's Judaean Desert, followed by Jordan and Egypt. I am also looking forward to organizing our trip to New Zealand and Australia. All promise to be exciting, but I can't wait that long. . . . After consulting my schedule, I circled three days in the following week, then confirmed that Carol and Mary could arrange the time to join me on my expedition.

I rubbed my hands together gleefully. I love it when a plan takes shape!

As the days passed, I used my spare time to search through a few of the other ancient sites created by my King, some with marvels of human interaction. I am fascinated by the architectural brilliance displayed within each individual chamber or room of this amazing King's palace. I, and now some of my family, have been able to see—especially now that I have found a means of exploring them in such fine detail. Only since making a conscious effort to closely observe and also attune my ears to *hear* the words spoken by the King, to have their essence *distilled into my soul*, have I truly learned to see through the veil separating—and now also combining—the physical and the spiritual.

This fresh capacity for discernment gives me access to the homeland of my Father's Kingdom, and it brings a deeper appreciation for the Word on which it is founded. Kartchner Caverns revealed to me how simply I may access all 66 palaces of the King. It brought me the satisfying assurance that wherever on earth I choose to be, I am free to roam and learn in the rooms of my Father's House, which encompasses all His palaces. I am free to study the King's blueprint for a long and satisfying life, and I have acquired the means of studying these Books of Life in such intricate detail it actually far supersedes the amazing holographic imagery I have been experiencing. I don't need a cave or even a specific place, as access is recorded in a single Guidebook volume telling of each of those 66 different palaces of the Kingdom.

We loaded my pickup and left early on Tuesday morning. I parked under a canopy of trees, and we hiked the five miles to the overhang above the river. We squeezed through the tunnel, dropped our backpacks in the cave, then went swimming in the cool, rippling river water. I showed my wife and daughter the opening to the tunnel leading to the underwater cavern, but we decided against using this entrance into the palace. We decided instead to access via the chamber of light—the index room, as it were—so we could explore room 17 before nightfall. We changed into dry clothes then started our adventure by following alongside the underground river to the crystal cave. It was all so new to the ladies, who wanted to stop and explore every nook and cranny, while I had to exercise some patience, as I was champing at the bit to get into the meat of our adventure.

I offered Carol the opportunity to twist the amethyst crystal to the right, and her delighted laughter rang through the cavern as the wall slid open. To ensure we all experienced the process together, we held hands and stepped across the threshold into the chamber of light. Perhaps I had become inured to the transition between worlds, and because Carol and Mary were experiencing this transition with me as their guide, there were only minor transitory effects, such as vertigo and the like. The door closed slowly behind us, emitting that gritty, crunching noise as it sealed us into the chamber of light. I strode purposefully across the room to the stone bench along the far wall. I was gripped with a feverish excitement, wanting to explore room 17, and felt a deep longing to share the anticipated celestial harmony of the angelic choir with Carol and Mary. Again, as I watched their excitement while they saw and absorbed, I realized how accustomed I had become to being in this place. It is a lot like a child being taught and trained in the transition processing of all life, first acquiring by use of the senses, then gaining understanding, and finally applying—a slow process, and a test of my patience.

I performed the necessary rituals that gave me access to the rooms of the 19th Palace while my wife and daughter watched silently. They were both totally transfixed by the pulsating Hebrew inscription that revealed the key to room 17. My palm vibrated, and my hand began to meld with the wall. My raised hand was followed by the portal opening to create a doorway into the room. On cue, we heard the harmony of voices in song as we stepped through the doorway: "Hear a just cause, O Lord; attend to my cry!"

It was a beautiful moment as we walked among a display of multiple holograms. Mary's face was filled with a radiant joy, her blue eyes sparkling with wonder, and Carol was clapping her hands with delight, like an innocent child in the embrace of her King. I drank in the scene, utterly thankful to my Lord, the King, who cloaked all three of us with His righteousness. Not only had He attended to my cry for salvation, but He kept my lips free of deceit, empowering me to share His Word and His Kingdom with all the world, especially those I love. Feeling safe beneath the shadow of a wing of a large metal bird suspended from the ceiling, I watched as they marveled at each little artifact they found—beautifully crafted wood and stone objects on the mantels, shelves, and tables within the room. Only a few of these included a human figure with a beating heart and moving lips, a nearby bed in a shadow box, an apple on a desk, a small chick under a hen's wing with a nearby lion behind a bush, and a pregnant woman holding the hand of another young child. As I joined, I felt my spirit surge within me, knowing I could call on my King at any moment—yet also having the simple assurance He often willingly chooses to answer or lead before I can think of asking. It gives me great peace knowing I can take refuge under His wings.

In times of great hardship when I have been emotionally distraught, my King wondrously showed His steadfast love and gave me refuge. Just as I treasure these precious women enjoined with me on this adventure, I know I am valuable and important to my King. He keeps me as the apple of His eye—the essential and all-important pupil allowing our seeing, but which also needs protection. I am so thankful for the righteousness my Lord has granted me, for it is this mantle that enables me to be certain I will gaze upon Him throughout eternity. Carol catches my eye, and we share a moment of unity that transcends the love of a husband and wife. We are children of the King, and our spirits soar as we drink deeply at this well of His Word.

We had planned to visit only one room before nightfall, but this palace is simply mesmerizing and none of us wants to leave, so we step through the doorway into the chamber of light where we can visit the next room. Mary asks if she can open the next doorway, and I'm pleased by her willingness to be actively involved in this palace intrigue. We all step up onto the stone bench, and I quickly talk her through the process. She begins by placing both palms on the wall, stepping slowly to her left. On her third step, a faint inscription is revealed between her palms, growing more vibrant with each pulse of light it emits. I peer over her shoulder, and I remember I must read the Hebrew right to left as I see the symbol for life, also representing the number 18: חי

She places her right palm over the number, murmuring softly as her hand starts vibrating. I watch as her hand melds with the wall. She pushes the portal wider then lifts her hand to complete the process, opening the doorway into yet another room in the King's 19th Palace. We all step through the doorway, met with the magnificent opening words of the rock-solid provision and protection of our King, sung in forte by the celestial choir: "I love you, O Lord, my strength. The Lord is my rock and my fortress and my deliverer, my God, my rock, in whom I take refuge, my shield, and the horn of my salvation, my stronghold." The room is large, with lots of ornate wooden furniture, tapestries, and finely woven rugs.

I am immediately reminded of many of the previous rooms I visited in this palace, but especially rooms 3 and 8, where my Lord showed to be my strength, my shield, my refuge, and my fortress. What I consider far more valuable, however, is the salvation He gave me, having saved me from the death that was the only end of "life" I knew. I was dead in my sins. He chose to lift me out of the overwhelming floodwaters—torrents of destruction so broad and varied, they terrified me. I was sinking in mire like quicksand before He brought me into His Kingdom. As the words of the song in this room sink into my consciousness like wakening from a dream, I'm glad there are no virtual-reality glasses here! Words alone are sufficient to depict the power and majesty of He who rides triumphally, flying swiftly on the wings of the wind. The words that fill

The King's 19th Palace

this room bring to mind the beautiful Christian hymn "On Christ the Solid Rock I stand"—so I start singing, in forte! I am filled with gratitude, for my hope is built on His Son's blood and righteousness—the solid Rock—not sinking sand!

The many words I have heard in the rooms of this palace, as well as numerous words within the King's other houses, have become my companions, lighting my lamp to dispel the darkness, enabling me to detect the right path and keep to it. Over time I have come to acknowledge this way of life the King has set before us is His perfect way, His perfect plan created, directed, and guided in every minute detail. While I keep to this righteous path, He gives me the strength and ability—like a mountain deer—to climb every height over any terrain. Similarly, as is evident in room 6 of the Ephesians house, He has also equipped me with impenetrable armor for every part of my being, and has given me strength for any battle I may face along this narrow path I walk. Carol and Mary stop what they are doing, and they join me as I lift my voice in praise to the King. We all sing, "Blessed be this King who is my rock, in whom is my salvation." Within this atmosphere, we all feel His presence strongly, and in our gratitude we spontaneously continue praising Him for rescuing us and lifting us high above all things as we sing, "Lift me higher, blessed Lord, our source of life and living water, far from sin and strife."

We exit room 18, and Mary closes the door behind us. We walk out to the overhang just in time to watch the sun slipping behind the horizon. I make a fire and we have dinner. I feel blessed by the goodness of God. We all go out to the overhang after dinner, and we are blown away by the beauty of the night sky. There is no moon visible, and the black sky is studded with innumerable stars projecting the artwork of our King, the grand Designer of this universe.

We rise early, and after a quick breakfast, we resume our exploration of the 19th Palace. This time Carol finds the inscription to room 19 and opens the doorway. We are greeted by the melodious sound of the celestial choir, and the opening line of their song reminds us all of last night's star-scape: "The heavens declare the glory of God, and the sky above proclaims his handiwork." As I enter this room, I remember how I first thought all creation silently witnessed and reflected the glory of the King; I now understand more fully, however, that all of creation "speaks" and the "words" are heard—the voice of creation goes out through all the earth. The words of creation we hear range from something as simple as the rustling wind waving fields of grain or moving through a canopy of trees to the crack of thunder following lightning.

Creation speaks through a myriad of sounds: tumbling rocks, gentle breezes or storm, raindrops, raging waters, and the cry of an eagle. Even the recordings of pulsars—from rapidly rotating and highly magnetized neutron stars—project real sound, the emitted pulsing radio waves and other electromagnetic radiation. Indeed, all nature and the universe sing, His glory to proclaim. This room is different in another way as we now are hearing all its words clearly being read to us.

We see how the stars declare the glory of God as we see a twinkling light-display in the night sky. Heat and light from the sun are also waveforms we sense as "communication." This same Light allows me not only to see as I read but to perceive as I am perceived by my King. As we explore deeper into this room, we "hear" and perceive with our senses all the words written in this room that include law, testimony, precepts, commandments—in fact to "hear" as we see and read the words of all the rooms of the houses in this Kingdom. I thank the Lord He has made me teachable, receptive, and desirous of His words—which are true, trustworthy, straightforward, pure, and perfectly complete in every way. These words not only "enlighten" me but are sweet upon my tongue with every taste. As I "digest" them, they are a source of sustenance but also protection to me, as I also feel His hand guiding my way (along the King's mighty and elevated "high-way").

The King's 19th Palace

Mary and Carol are exploring the fine details of the room, feeling the luxurious silk hangings on the walls and tracing with their delicate fingers the intricate patterns carved into the wooden cabinets. My heart swells with love for these magnificent beings, who have wholeheartedly thrown themselves into this adventure so they, too, may grow closer to our King. I find a comfortable armchair to sit in, and I continue listening to all these words as I contemplate the mysteries of this glorious Kingdom. I pray that all the words that come forth from my mouth—as well as the thoughts in my heart—might truly be in accord with the King in every way, and acceptable in His sight because He truly is my Rock and my Redeemer. I feel a hand on my shoulder. I open my eyes and realize I have been meditating for some time. My companions are ready to move on to the next room. Carol finds the next inscription along the stone bench and places her palm over the glowing Hebrew letter כ

She involuntarily experiences a sharp intake of breath as her hand begins to vibrate then slowly begins to meld with the wall. She turns to me, and I see the wonder in her eyes. Carol was greatly intrigued when I first told her about this manner by which I had gained access to the King's 19th Palace, so she spent a few hours asking for more details. She had expressed a wish to experience the same feeling—of becoming one with the architecture of this palace—and now I have the exquisite privilege of watching her dream unfold. She widens the portal slightly then raises her left hand to pull the door open, and we all three enter. I have a sense as I enter this 20th room that the Lord has been preparing me to become more aware of all He has provided. Mary is the first to find the virtual-reality glasses, calling Carol and I over to a table in the corner of the room. I encourage Mary to put them on, and as she does, a second pair appears. Carol claps her hands with delight, and I gesture for her to try them on. A third pair appears, and I place them on the bridge of my nose.

I am immediately transported to a battlefield, seeing Carol and Mary also near me, and I realize I am in an army uniform. I gain a sudden but intense understanding of how thoroughly able my King is, and it fills me with courage. I clench my fists, knowing He gives me the ability to fight each upcoming battle because I am faithfully conscripted into His army. Everyone I see is an equipped foot soldier. I also see many horses hooked to chariots to one edge, but they are all tied up with no one near. I am also aware of being surrounded by an army of Kingdom soldiers, thoroughly trained, battle-hardened, and ready to effectuate the King's cause. Together we will carry forth our King's ultimate desire and plant His flag. I see a warrior holding the King's flagstaff, its flag snapping in the crisp breeze atop the wooden staff, which is etched with curious designs. I am awash with His divine presence, and unable to curb my enthusiasm, I start singing, "His banner over me is love." Others may have confidence in their chariots and horses, but I have confidence in the strength of my King. As my first song ends, I start singing, "Praise forever to the King of kings."

I take the glasses off to see Mary is high-fiving Carol—they have also removed their glasses. The words of the choir resonate around the room: "May He grant you your heart's desire and fulfill all your plans!" Mary turns: "Dad, there is a wooden door against the far wall. Do you think we can open it? I want to see what's on the other side."

"Ah, yes! My past experience of wooden doors in the rooms of this palace has proved to reveal shortcuts between adjoining rooms."

"That makes sense," Carol interjects. "See, the number 21 is carved into the wood."

"In English?" I ask, rising from my armchair.

"No, in Roman numerals," Mary replies.

"Interesting. That's a first." I trace the numerals with my forefinger. "Let's have a look." I turn the handle, and the door is actually

The King's 19th Palace

the entire wall as it opens quietly, revealing a connected room. We are greeted by an army surrounding its enemies, bringing them bound before a blazing fire, where they seem to disappear. I am reminded I can face the battles of this day and every day—just as King David trusted in the Lord, so do I. Through the steadfast love of the Most High, I shall not be moved, for my King has given me my heart's desire. I feel prepared and have nothing to fear—He keeps me from evil and holds every aspect of the future. I begin to sing, "Because He lives, I can face tomorrow. . . ."

Carol finds another internal door, leading to room 22. We enter the room, but none of us are prepared for the heart-wrenching words being uttered and sung: "My God, my God, why have you forsaken me? Why are you so far from saving me, from the words of my groaning?" We are silent as we stand just inside the doorway of this powerfully prophetic room. I see a stiff-backed wooden chair, where I sit as a play proceeds on a stage. I contemplate the deep prophetic meaning encompassed within the continuing words spoken by the actors. Their words and actions describe the enormity of what the King's Son suffered on my behalf so many years ago. The immense detail of King David's vision of the cross is astounding, including the evildoers who encircled Jesus and how they pierced His hands and feet. The words now recount how His garments were divided among them and how they cast lots for His clothing.

Now the words are a minor key song that laments the pain and sorrow of moments that occurred in my distant past—yet King David envisaged his Lord's suffering more than a thousand years before it happened. I am astonished at the accuracy of his prophecy, even though it is only a brief summary of the events removing our Messiah from dwelling with us in His human form! He was my "Suffering Servant." I feel His presence in this room, which prompts my soul to sing, "In this very room."

I sit stiffly engrossed in sober reflection, but Carol and Mary want to continue exploring—they have found another wooden door. Mary opens the door, and I recognize room 23, which Carol and I accessed in Kartchner Caverns. My heart beats faster as the fluid nature of this Kingdom sinks into my conscious mind—we are able to enter any room we desire to perceive, from anywhere in the world, as long as we seek His Kingdom first. The angelic choir sings the opening verse underpinning this room: "The Lord is my shepherd; I shall not want. He makes me lie down in green pastures." Mary and Carol explore the room while I sit on the threshold, singing softly with the choir. I pull out my old journal and open it to where I have made a note about rooms 22, 23, and 24. It is an alliteration sequence of three one-word summaries describing the essence of each room from three different perspectives, but all concern the King's Son, who is also called Christ or Deliverer.

My wife and daughter return from their exploration of room 23, so I close my journal, and we step through the doorway back into room 22.

Chapter 8

Lift up your gates—lift up your doors, that the King of glory may come in. I lift up my soul. O my God, in you I trust; let me not be put to shame; let not my enemies triumph over me! (based on Psalm 24:7 and 25:1–2). Our King takes our times of sorrow and tears and turns them to joy.

Mary and Carol continue exploring room 22, marveling at the artifacts scattered about the room. I change to a more comfortable armchair in the corner of the room and pull out my journal again. I am keen to bring to remembrance the themes I have penned that sum up the essential building blocks of the room we are in, as well as the adjacent two rooms. The sequence of summaries describes three perspectives on the King's Son, tying in connections to Christ our only Deliverer. Room 22 depicts Christ as Savior, room 23 as Shepherd, and room 24 as Sovereign. Another sequence reveals Him through His Grace in 22, as Guide in 23, and He who radiates the Father's Glory in 24. The third sequence of these three rooms illustrates the power of Christ through the Cross, the Crook, and the Crown.

My thoughts turn again to room 23. What a powerful collection of images permeate the writing that underpins the construction of this room. It is a room I have known since childhood. I came to love and understand this room so much more fully when reading it nightly with my first wife, Gini, during our battle with the brain cancer that ultimately took her to the mansion room our King had prepared for her. A soft sigh escapes me, but a second later my mood is lifted by the sound of Carol's laughter. She is pointing to something on a shelf, and Mary puts one hand on Carol's shoulder as they both chuckle delightedly. It is a bittersweet moment displaying but one of the many instances in life that are a mixture of sorrow and joy—I am experiencing sad reflection quickly switched to a moment of humble gratitude for the blessings my King constantly pours out upon my life.

Back to my thoughts that turn to dreamland. Because of my Shepherd (the King's Son), I recognize I am like a sheep—I will not lack pasture, nor water, and I am confident of being kept on the correct path. I love that the water is still—sheep are afraid of fast-moving water, for it can be too turbulent to drink from, but still water moves gently. It is pure to drink and not stagnant. I will not fear any evil because He is near me and protecting me. I know He will also lead me through that valley of the shadow—that death is conquered and instantaneously I will go from life to life. I will dwell forever with my Shepherd, who loves me and provides for me, leading me through every day and in every way. It's an awesome feeling to once again recall His power and beauty contained within this room.

My focus changes to room 24 as I visualize a similar concept to the fencing I saw bordering the King's land (including my own portion) in room 16. I lift my eyes to see atop a high hill. A difficult ascent leads to a walled castle with its "gates" and "ancient doors" provided by the King to keep dangerous people out but also as a means of protection for those within. I see people walking up that steep and holy hill, stopping to wash their hands. I also sense somehow they must have a pure heart, for I know those who come to the entrance asking for the gates to be lifted up must know who this King of Glory truly is (one of many names referencing the King's Son). For He is the One whom I see leading through the gate everyone the King has chosen—He will usher in all those His Father allows into His Kingdom. My eyes open again, and I realize Carol and Mary are ready to move to the next room. We exit room 22, and this time I open the door to room 25.

We enter the room, and the choir-song greets us with the opening verse, which sets the tone for upholding the construction of this room as I hear the word "lift" now applying to me: "To you, O Lord, I lift up my soul. O my God, in you I trust." I also begin to sing based on the pattern of this room: "Unto Thee O King do I lift up my soul, in Thee do I trust. Do not let me be ashamed, let not my enemies triumph over me. Make me know Thy paths, teach me Your ways. Remember not the sins of my youth." I live my life filled with confidence, knowing the King is good and upright. He instructs me in my every step and has even removed the guilt I once carried like a heavy backpack. It's such a comfort knowing I can lift up my soul to the King. I will continue to learn what He teaches me.

Thinking back on my life before meeting the King, I stand amazed He even allowed me through the gate to enter His Kingdom. Then I remember, my King has given me a new heart and put His Spirit within me that I might give Him honor and praise; my sin has been pardoned and I am freed from guilt all because of what Christ (my King) has accomplished for me on His cross. All the paths of the Lord demonstrate His steadfast love and faithfulness. I now dwell in the house of the Lord; my soul shall abide in well-being, and my offspring shall inherit the land. I look at Mary, who is running her forefinger along the spine of a large, leather-bound book. It gives me great comfort knowing His chosen among my children and grandchildren will ultimately be welcomed by the King. The friendship of the Lord is mine because I have absolute reverence for Him, and He makes known to me His covenant.

The King's 19th Palace

"What a Friend We Have in Jesus" is a song swirling in my mind—what a continuing joy seeing so many rooms include verses of songs of praise to the King as well.

Mary, sensing my fond gaze, looks up and catches my eye. She sees the love in my eyes, and we smile as she speaks, "I'd like to show John and Elizabeth this room. I want them to be aware of their inheritance."

"Yes," I agree, "I'd like to bring the whole family to see the 19th Palace from this special entranceway."

"How does it work, Dad? How were we able to see rooms in this palace both from Kartchner Caverns and here in the Appalachian foothills? It's mind-boggling!"

"I think we or anyone whom our King chooses can enter any of the King's 66 palaces and their rooms from anywhere in the world, and I suspect we're not bound to enter only through caves and caverns alone. . . . In truth, I don't really know how it works, but I'm hoping to experiment more with this theory once I'm back home." Carol joins us, and we agree to move on to the next room. Mary leads the way, and Carol takes the initiative now, stepping up onto the stone bench. She moves purposefully to her left with outstretched arms, her hands sliding along the wall. An inscription brightens as she places her palm over the Hebrew symbol for the number 26, progressing to the doorway opening. We enter the room to the sound of singing of the opening verse that gives the room its structure, its meaning, and its perceived message of advice and counsel for my life's journey: "Vindicate me, O Lord, for I have walked in my integrity, and I have trusted in the Lord without wavering or slipping."

As I step into the room, I immediately see an ornately carved table and placed on its surface is a pair of virtual-reality glasses. I pick them up and put them on, as I see Mary and Carol doing the same. A courtroom scene appears before me. I think I am walking the straight and narrow, but various tests I have failed are listed on a board. I see I am guilty, no chance to leave the prison of my sin, as I stand pleading before the judge—who is also the King. Since being welcomed into the Kingdom, I have been striving to walk in truth—at least, as much as I possibly could. I have trusted in His Word and His help. I'm not like the wicked group described in room 1: I do not sit with men who think, speak, and act in falsehood, nor do I consort with hypocrites. I hate the assembly of evildoers, and I refuse to sit with the wicked. The King releases me to walk out in freedom and joy. I love living in the house of the Lord, in the place where His glory dwells. Throughout the balance of my days, I will strive to walk steadily on level ground, striding confidently in the truth; and with all that is within me, I will bless His holy name. As I view myself walking away from the judgment seat through the virtual-reality glasses, my real self—the man wearing the glasses—starts chanting a specific refrain repeatedly: "Free because of Thee, I am walking free, not in a prison locked. Onward I will walk on level ground!"

We all agree to call it a day, feeling pleased with the progress we have made. Because this is still so new to Carol and Mary, we spend more time exploring as I also describe the crystal cave on our return journey. Once they have sated their curiosity, we return to our home base. We leave our daypacks in the cave and head out to the overhang. Again, it seems we have been gone much longer than our watches now show—there is about an hour of daylight left, so we collect firewood, and I make a fire when we return to the cave. I cook over the coals while Carol prepares a salad. I add wood to the fire after dinner, and we lie as comfortably as possible, discussing the rooms we have visited and how the meaning and application we extract from them is increased by our detailed exploration. Carol sets an alarm, so we will wake early to continue our journey of exploration.

I am awake before Carol's alarm sounds, but I lie quietly, thanking my King for giving His people such detailed instruction on

The King's 19th Palace

how we might live a long and satisfying life. His goodness knows no bounds. I hear the rustle of a sleeping bag, and when I turn my head, Mary kisses her palm then blows me a good-morning kiss. The alarm sounds and we rise. Carol and I decide to take a short walk before breakfast, but Mary is hungry, so she starts preparing an omelet for our return. Carol and I sit on a large boulder along the river's edge. I tell Carol how grateful I am to God for placing her in my life. She looks at me questioningly, knowing I have more to say.

"I had a moment's sadness yesterday while exploring room 23. Gini and I drank in the words of that psalm every night after receiving her deadly diagnosis—and I was thinking of you losing your Everett also." Carol lays a gentle hand on my forearm. I cover her hand with my own, and we sit in silence for a moment. "I'm okay. . . . I know, like your husband, she is safe and secure in the presence of our King, joyously blessed beyond measure."

"Your moment of sadness is perfectly understandable, Gene. I suppose only the loss of a child could bring greater sadness than losing a life partner."

"Yes. I suppose so." I turn to Carol and brush her cheek with the back of my fingers. "The thing is, in that moment, God allowed me to feel the sadness—but before the feeling enveloped me, He reminded me of the beauty that still fills my life. . . . He takes our times of sorrow and tears, turning them to joy." Carol tilts her head to one side, evidently curious about my meaning. "Almost immediately after experiencing that sadness, I heard your laugh ringing through the room. Then you and Mary were both laughing together, and I realized my sadness was on my own behalf. I knew Gini was eternally secure in her heavenly abode, and that God sent you to me to help me complete my own journey, and for you to have my help completing your journey without Everett . . . to the place where there are no more tears." My wife shifted closer and leaned her head on my shoulder.

"Our great King gave us to one another, so we could both finish the work He started in us.[6] We are all blessed beyond measure. We serve the Most High God, who created the heavens and the earth." We sit quietly for another moment, drinking in the sun and the warmth of our God-granted love for each other.

As we approach the overhang, the delicious smell of garlic and onion reaches us, and I realize I'm ravenous. Mary adds the beaten eggs to the pan, and within minutes we are served a gourmet omelet upon a coal-toasted slice of bread. After breakfast we pray and dedicate the day to our heavenly Father, asking His blessing and protection over us and our family members. I place a kettle of water above the coals, and ten minutes later I serve freshly brewed coffee. We're officially ready to start today's adventure!

We make rapid progress through the intermediate stages of our journey to the chamber of light now that they have absorbed the wonders of the crystal cave. Mary steps up onto the bench and quickly opens the portal then the doorway to room 27. No matter how many times I am greeted by the celestial song of each room, in room 27, I am filled with the immense beauty of the opening verse—it strikes a visceral chord within my being: "The Lord is my light and my salvation; whom shall I fear? The Lord is the stronghold of my life; of whom shall I be afraid?"

We enter the room. Carol and Mary start wandering around, but I stand in the entranceway, paying close attention to the words being sung. I begin to hum along with the melody, recognizing important moments in my own life being reflected somehow back to me. While I do not understand all in this spiritual or internal dimension, I am amazed at my feelings and impressions. Something like a dream or the Old Testament visions I have read about. One thing I have asked from the King, something I keep seeking, is that I may live in His house all the days of my life, to gaze on His

---

6. See Philippians 1:6.

beauty. I hear these concepts being sung to me by the angelic choir, and they fill my heart and inner being with gladness. I sing along with the choir as they start again at the opening verse, and in my heart I renew my vow to search out continually more of what the King reveals to me in all the houses in this Kingdom. He teaches me His way and guides me along a level path. I know our spouses are at home and at peace with our Father, and I take courage from the words that fill this room: "I believe that I shall look upon the goodness of the Lord in the land of the living!" I renew my vow to always wait for and on the Lord. I will be strong, and I will let my heart take courage while I wait for the Lord! I will not act without His sure guidance.

We spend a good while in this room, and once all three of us have received the distinct feeling of the blessings sensed, we naturally start thanking our almighty King for giving us His Word. We are still singing His praises as I close the door behind us. As Mary opens the doorway to the adjacent room 28, the opening verse of a song reminds me of the initial image I had of a massive cornerstone rising from the bedrock: "To you, O Lord, I call; my rock, be not deaf to me, lest, if you be silent to me, I become like those who go down to the pit." Our Rock speaks! It seems like such a long time has passed since that first revelation I received about this precious cornerstone—of the Messiah as the Cornerstone, the Bedrock of this awe-inspiring Kingdom who graciously adds us as living stones building the Father's house. I am so utterly grateful I am no longer going down to the pit. I have been redeemed! I watch Mary and Carol, each woman fully engaged with the message presented in this room. I say a prayer of thanks to my King, and while I pray, I wait upon Him to reveal the fresh mysteries of His Kingdom we know are interwoven into the fabric and tapestries we see all around in this very room. My mind processes the phrase "to wait upon the King," and while I recognize I am thinking of "waiting" in terms of being *patient*, the sense of *serving* also arises in my mind!

I consider the many ways in which He has blessed me, and I linger lovingly on special moments in my life legacy that only He could have provided, like my three children, my foster, and now stepchildren, and all the additional grand- and great-grandchildren—as well as the countless people He has allowed me to interact with. In this moment of praise, I realize I am blessing my King by recounting—in absolute wonder and thankfulness—all of His responses, not only to my every need but also to my godly desires. His excellent provision for me fills me with gratitude, and it strikes me that a substantial portion of this provision includes His hearing my prayers and His appropriate response. This room has allowed me to not only see my past and enjoy this present, but to know the eternal future I have been granted. He is my strength and protection, and it is *He* who changed my heart, so I am fully at liberty to trust and serve Him.

Knowing the vast number of rooms in this 19th Palace, we decide to continue our exploration, and we are all singing along with the choir as we enter room 29. Yet again we are all three immediately drawn to this room by the power of the opening verse of song: "Ascribe to the Lord, O heavenly beings, ascribe to the Lord glory and strength." I sense and begin seeing the heavenly host establishing the essence of this room—by proclaiming the Word of our King—enacting the very words they proclaim! With my glasses, I first see mighty waves of the sea roaring as loud thunder sounds. Then the scene changes to a loud sound with a whirlwind or tornado breaking down a large swath of cedar forest followed by huge flames erupting in a gigantic orange fireball, and I feel the shaking of the ground beneath. All nature is ascribing to the King glory and strength. We are then instructed to give or render to the Lord all the glory due His name. All then turns quiet and I feel at peace.

I turn again to thoughts of blessing, honoring, and praising the King (instead of requests and expecting Him to bless me). I am blessed to be a blessing! These thoughts tie in as I contemplate how truly majestic this King of Glory is. How appropriate that I am to address my all-powerful King as, "His Majesty!" He speaks and all creation responds. I am part of His creation. He is in charge and in command of absolutely every detail, whether storm or calm. I see the reverence Carol and Mary show as they view and study the intricate details of this room. I am overwhelmed by gratitude to my King for being able to share His Word with my family and all the world.

Chapter 9

His Word is put within my heart as a fire, a fire I cannot keep within. I am to be like a branding iron plucked from that hot fire and used to impress upon others our King's searing brand of truth (based on Jeremiah 20:9 and Zechariah 3:1–2).

We are back to the cave just before sunset and eat a light picnic at the river. The setting sun paints a masterpiece of pastel pink, red, and orange hues across the western skyline. We collect firewood on our way back to the overhang, and when we reach the cave, I make a fire. Carol sets her alarm for our early morning drive back home, and the ladies both snuggle into their sleeping bags early while I sit at the fireside. I'm not sleepy just yet, so I make tea, then I stoke the fire and add some wood to it. I put a blanket beside me, lean back on a comfortable rock, sitting and gazing into the flames. Before long I am mesmerized by the range of yellow, orange, and blue firelight sparking and flickering into the cool cavern air. The flames make me drowsy, and my contentment elicits a feeling of extreme gratitude for being able to share the beauty and truth of my King's 19th Palace. The words of a song pop into my mind, and I sing softly while staring into the dancing firelight: "I lift my hands to the coming King, to the Great I Am, to You I sing...."

The King's 19th Palace

I grow increasingly drowsy as I try to work my way through a few verses of the song—then I start humming, unable to collect my thoughts sufficiently to sing the next verse. I hum for what seems to be no more than a minute when the flames suddenly shift into a deeper intensity, creating a soft violet edge along the flickering tongues of blue flame. I watch, fascinated, as an opening appears in the midst of the flames, and I feel drawn to explore what lies beyond the shimmering firelight. I rise softly, not wanting to wake the sleeping. The flames open up as I approach, and my body absorbs the heat as though it were spring sunshine, my focus fixed on the door that appears beyond. I step effortlessly through the flames and turn the handle—the door opens easily. I step into a hallway with a marble floor, and as I do, I experience the strangest synesthetic sensation. I hear the angelic choir singing; the words seem to be flickering as they create many rooms connected to this central hall. But as I stand in the doorway of the first room, instead of now hearing the words—I perceive and feel them as shimmering words of light tumbling through the air, which are then absorbed into the very fabric of my being.

I laugh spontaneously, excited at this novel sensation. It's quite invigorating to be filled with these powerful words, so skillfully stitched together in my mind by my King. I noted the number 30 on the door when I walked through that fiery doorway, then followed by an experience so similar to our recent visit in room 29, hearing the voice of the King flashing forth flames of fire. The words I am taking in confirm a progression from the previous room, ascribing to the Lord the glory due His name, which encourages me to continue exulting my King. I feel Him lifting me up from the pit of mire and mud. He has given me new life as I am gently placed in His Kingdom. The edges of this room are soft and hazy, as if a warm mist is drifting through it, carrying the words on its vaporous wings. These words touch my heart and sink deep—I am momentarily reminded of the grief and sorrow we sometimes experience in life—but for we who follow the King, there is always restoration. He rescues us to life, separating us from among those who go down to the pit. He has spared my soul from the horrors of hell.

I am dreaming it is evening, and I am feeling somewhat sad (and sometimes even weep), followed by a night of tossing and turning—but now at dawn and the break of a new day, I perceive my present changed and true condition, and I erupt in joyful shouting. I realize I have the favor of the King forever and will never be cast out. There can be no greater reason for my exultation! A phalanx of fiery words marches purposefully toward my soul, and I open my arms wide to receive them: "You have turned for me my mourning into dancing; you have loosed my sackcloth and clothed me with gladness, that my glory may sing your praise and not be silent. O Lord my God, I will give thanks to you forever!"[7]

As I exit the room, I take a few steps to the next door along the hallway and cross the threshold through a door displaying brass numerals: 31. I see a splendid leather armchair with a footstool along the far wall, and like the previous room, this one also has hazy edges, as if the walls are shimmering bands of energy. I sit in the soft light of this room to think and pray while my mind adjusts to this strange phenomenon. I am chilled, so I pull up the lap blanket, feeling safe and protected in this environment. I know my King is truly my fortress, my hiding place—it feels like I am being hidden in the cleft of an enormous rock. My majestic King is my security, irrespective of whether I feel happy, disappointed, or distressed. I relax into the armchair, soaking up the visible words being drawn into my soul. My mind drifts, focusing briefly on random events I have experienced throughout my life.

Though I may sometimes wonder if anything I have accomplished in my life has been any good—or has produced any good—even that very thought, that specific concern, is not my own

---

7. Psalm 30:11–12

judgment or doing. Instead, I am being held in the King's hands, and in Him I place my complete trust. As I process this nugget of truth, knowing my King is good and does good, I realize this reminder is also written in room 119, item 68. I recognize the need to allow my mind some clear focus, so I can truly accept I am one of the King's beloved. "Oh, how I love Him, because He first loved me" and "He's got the whole world in His hands" are lyrics floating in my head!

I rise from the armchair and cross directly opposite into room 32—I walk or seem to float straight into it. As I enter, a blessed relief washes over me—the words that pierce my soul delight me to my core—my sin has been taken away. Following my elation, I suddenly feel faint and weak as I recall my past sins. Just as the words of this room flood my being with strength, so does a range of images flood my mind with remorse. It's hard to believe I was once quite a different man—I used to worship so many of the bad and ugly things of the world. My spirit cringes when I think about all the lifeless and rotten ideas hidden deep within that lifeless heart. My spell of weakness continues, and I sweat as I toss and turn, wrestling with those hard vestiges of my past. I am no longer to think sinful thoughts. I will speak no guileful words nor perform any wicked actions.

The words of this room concerning thought, word, and deed flow through me like a cool breeze, relieving my troubled soul as I remember what the King's Son did for me on the cross. I raise my voice in song: "To my King be the glory, great things He has done." I am at peace as I am reminded that, the moment I pledged allegiance to the King of glory, He gave me a true and complete pardon. Immediately after giving me a new, transplanted heart, He led me through the "life-gate" into this Kingdom on that wonderful day. It is still so hard to comprehend how, in my human frailty, my sinful ways continue . . . and yet they are covered—but at the same time, they are not hidden from the King. In these rooms and in the many other houses in this Kingdom, my Father the King, through His Holy Spirit, continues to teach me and give me counsel. He has given me discernment of right and wrong, thus I strive daily to have less need to be guided and reined in like a bridled horse.

From the soft, hazy edge of the room, I see a well-constructed string of words flowing toward me. They are hot and seem to pierce to my core as if by a branding iron fresh from fire: "Many are the sorrows of the wicked, but steadfast love surrounds the one who trusts in the Lord. Be glad in the Lord, and rejoice, O righteous, and shout for joy, all you upright in heart!" As I prepare to leave this room, I sing about the redemption I have received, and I thank the King for His life-gate, constructed before the foundation of the earth, allowing His children to enter into His Kingdom. I truly am blessed as I rejoice in His goodness, in the life-giving mercy of my King, as I feel myself turn right in the hallway and into room 33.

As I enter, my soul is once again saturated with the presence of my King—He who loves righteousness and justice. The words that stream into and fill my heart reiterate a concept that I now see flowing throughout the rooms of this 19th Palace: the earth is full of the *steadfast love* of the Lord. I bask in His wonderful presence, and although I have just recently lifted my voice in song, the fiery words that enter my soul now encourage me to sing a new song—one of my own thought and writing. I fill my lungs with fresh breath and render my new song to the King: "I give thanks to my Father, and praise to Him is befitting; He has given me His Word of truth. His truth is at work in my heart, that righteous heart He has put within me. By His spoken word, all of creation came about, all people and nations. In this Kingdom I reside—truly blessed am I, along with all the other adopted sons He has chosen." No rhyme, no meter, just truth ringing as a melody in my soul. Feeling His steadfast love upon me, I am floating back into the hallway.

I am now walking across the hall, and as I step boldly into room 34, I see a pair of special glasses on a wrought-iron desk.

I put them on, and I once again have the ability to witness scenes of virtual reality. I am immediately prompted to go through a side archway, finding myself in a garden where I join with others to bless and praise the King for all He has done. I have a fleeting picture of room 23 with its feast table, as I now see another feast set out before of us. We are all seated, and having thanked our King for the banquet, we are encouraged to "Taste and see that the Lord is good!" Never have I encountered such scintillating flavors, and yet again I must declare how good the King truly is. I clean my plate to the very edges as I savor the last bite.

I sit quietly, satisfied and replete, and I begin to take in the Lord with all my other senses. The banquet table disappears, and the scene shifts gear as we turn our attention to one of the princes. He entertains us with a true, nail-biting story of how he once had to engage his wiles and use his God-given senses to escape certain death. He tells us how he changed his behavior, pretending to be crazy in the presence of another king, all the time praying the deception would work. His ruse *did* work, and his life was spared yet again. He ends his story by heaping praise upon our King. Then I see and hear many more people sharing their broken lives, recounting the various evil ways they used to practice and the vile manner in which they once lived. Many tears are shed as they speak of how they were downcast and downtrodden before the King appeared on the scene of their life and how He, too, provided deliverance for them to enter into this Kingdom. We all lift our voices as one, joyfully praising Him together for ransoming us, for providing this awesome refuge.

I return the glasses to the wrought-iron desk before exiting the room. I turn to my left, and according to the pattern of the hallway, instead of entering the next room to the left, I cross the hall to the opposite side. I enter a room displaying the numeral 35 on the door, as well as a specific label: "My King is my Deliverer." I immediately recognize this room is arranged as a theater, and I feel the sense of safety it brings to me. I have no need for glasses, as I am brought up onto the stage. I see my inward thoughts, coupled with knowing and reciting my directed lines, which reflect parts of my life as a written and choreographed play. I see many past times of deep difficulty and distress from various kinds of enemies—whether internal or external, people or circumstances. Each time the King equips me to fend for myself, and He also valiantly defends me, driving my enemies away like chaff before the wind. Stage left I witness a phalanx of fiery words marching determinedly, this time to my defense. The angel of the Lord drives away my enemies, pursuing them off stage beyond the borders of my safe haven. I *know* my King has my back. This fact brings me great reassurance. My Defender provides both armament and a plan to keep me safe. I am thankful for my "big D" as I sing "songs of deliverance."

Filled with a sense of peace, I seem to float directly into room 36, and again, flames of words are floating about the room, bringing to mind the deep reverence I have for the King. Yet the more time I spend in His Kingdom, the more I have come to realize that mixed with this reverence is a deep dread of disrespecting or even disappointing my King. The floating words are actually building this room and are a stark reminder of why I constantly choose to revere my King. I see a long line of milestones disappearing into the far distant corner, and the hazy edges of the room give the appearance of these milestones drifting off into infinity. I realize they mark the journey of many enemies who—being totally deceived—did not fear the King. I call them enemies, for they are somehow not chosen to be sharing in this Kingdom as joint heirs with the King's Son.

All the milestones lead to an area of darkness that obscures the space beyond the soft-edged wall, creating a stark abyss, devoid of light. I steer my floating body clear of this section, and as I continue to another part of the room, I am reminded of why I am not afraid but rather filled with peace—my King is the Light! He has provided me with light to see, both physically and spiritually—giving me the

The King's 19th Palace

ability to feel and see His loving care. Just like standing beside a fire or feeling the full sun on my skin, His Word brings warmth and light to my heart and mind. He is teaching me to fully grasp how much He loves me, even as He deals with my inward pride, my waywardness, and the wickedness of my very being—which because of my human condition is often expressed outwardly. How precious is His steadfast love! I take refuge in the shadow of His wings, as He gives me drink from the river of His delights. My King is the fountain of life and the source of all light.

Energized and invigorated, I head diagonally across the hall and enter room 37. The words that skip and flitter about this room bring a child's song to mind: "A, B, C, D, E, F, G—H, I, J, K, L, M, N, O P . . ." I wonder why this alphabet song from my childhood has come to me—and then I make the connection: the writings and décor of this room represent one of the Old Testament acrostic writings favored by the Hebrews—each item line begins with a letter of the Hebrew alphabet in a specific order. Since first finding the entrance to the King's 19th Palace here in the caverns within the Appalachian foothills, I have been studying the Hebrew alphabet and numerical system, so I am able now to make some sense of the poetic features. As I am reading the words of each line, they are like flames of fire proceeding from first to last. This room creates a composition that cumulatively describes wicked people and wickedness of every sort, but once this scene has been depicted, I as the reader am instructed to wait upon the Lord, seeing that the wicked will have their day of judgment. I know my steps are established, but now I stumble and am falling. I do not hit the ground, however, and I am instead lifted up again to the straight and narrow path.

I leave the room, knowing my King is my stronghold in the time of trouble and that He delivers me from the wicked because I take refuge in Him. I cross the hall and step into room 38, but as I cross the threshold, I perceive a disgusting smell. I look around, perplexed, but then I realize I am the source of this terrible stench!

I stink of my own doing. I have been oblivious—how could I have ignored this simply awful condition? The burning words that hotly fill my soul bring me to the realization that despite the grace I have received I continue to offend my King. Embarrassed by my sinful condition I am carrying like a backpack on my shoulders, I recognize I am justly deserving of any discipline He may choose. We sometimes speak of a "sound mind" and "sound body," but I have neither....

He created me and knows absolutely everything about me. There is nothing hidden. In fact, I walk around carrying an increasingly heavy burden of my own making, seeking ways to find relief but without going to the King, which is the crux of the problem. It seems as if everyone and everything is against me, even my friends and family seem to be keeping me at a distance. Not only was I not smelling the rot; I am not seeing or hearing solutions, mostly because of my own sin. I need to lose my self-pity and the self-destructive thoughts that only open new wounds because they too will fester with time. I am shaken to the core, horrified now by the cumulative effect prevalent in all these rooms adjacent to this hallway. This is a powerful lesson learned, and I make a firm decision: going forward I will seek help from my King. I have been laboring under an incorrect impression—my King is not distant nor removed, as I have wrongly perceived. He is in this very place! I confess and am genuinely sorry for my sin. The warm mist in this room turns to searing heat delivering words into my being, this time like flaming darts, and I am grateful to leave this room and its stench.

My legs tremble slightly as I move hesitantly into the hallway, uncertain of where to turn. I hear a new sound, one I have heard before, but my mind is grappling to place it. I feel someone shaking me and I open my eyes. A smiling face looms above me with hair disheveled. "Dad, you're whimpering. Were you dreaming? You must have fallen asleep at the fire." Carol switches off her alarm, and the sound is gone. I heave a troubled sigh, thankful to be awake in the cave with family. Carol and Mary sense my unease, and they leave me to my thoughts as they head off through the morning mist to the river to splash a little water on their faces. I rekindle the fire still shooting occasional sparks, feeling more at ease. What a night! I am flooded again with images from the rooms along the hallway, and in spite of my sobering ordeal in room 38, I am grateful for the experience. I recall the awful stench emanating from my carnal self, and I decide to join the ladies at the river.

    I am about to squeeze through the tunnel to the overhang when I stop. I go to my backpack to retrieve my biodegradable shower gel. I chuckle softly as I make my way to the water. My King was teaching me even in my sleep as I dreamed, but now in the light of day I feel I was as wide awake as I have ever been.

Chapter 10

In every room you see and hear the words of that specific palace room presented in so many interesting and exciting ways—so you must listen carefully to understand. God imparts into your inmost being a portion of His wisdom through your understanding and application of His presented Word (based on Romans 10:16–17, 20).

We drive away from the foothills, stopping at Mary's to spend some time with Elizabeth and John. When Carol and I arrive home, we clean our camping gear, catch up on routines, and eat an early dinner. Encouraged by my "dreamy" experience by the fire last night, I have been meaning to try a new entering approach into the 19th Palace, so when Carol turns in early, I decide to test my theory. Knowing I have acquired the means of studying many of the King's other palaces in their physically constructed forms, I now want to test the range of accessibility open to me. Studying these Books of Life in intricate holographic detail has given me great insight into the King's blueprint for living a satisfying life, but as much as I have enjoyed the "traveling" process of these adventures, I only have limited time to explore caves.

I want to visit room 39, the next room in the sequence of the 19th Palace, so I sit in my comfortable armchair in my lounge with my Bible—and note, I have one volume of *The Chronicles of Narnia*

The King's 19th Palace

sitting on the end table next to a lamp. I focus on the closed door of the linen closet. I close my eyes and bring to mind the Hebrew numerals that convey the number: על

In my mind's eye, I see these numerals burnt into the center of the door, and everything changes. The door to the linen closet is no longer painted white—it is a dark, wooden door with an ornate brass handle. The Hebrew numerals are glowing softly as they pulsate, growing brighter and dimmer between pulsations. My breathing and heart rate are no longer relaxed. *Can it be this simple?* I am rising and walk to the door, noticing the walls of my lounge have taken on a hazy look, as though made from shimmering bands of energy. I sense the familiar vibration, and my hand easily opens the door using the brass handle.

Thinking about my experience concerning the stench of our sinful human condition, I proceed cautiously, aware of my beating heart as I step through the doorway. Again, angelic voices greet me, but before I can tune in to their song, I see a battery of words floating purposefully toward me, and the sound of the choir dissipates as I focus on the words. I tilt my head slightly to read them: "I will guard my ways, that I may not sin with my tongue; I will guard my mouth as with a muzzle." I realize the choir is almost muted—just the slightest sound now—but rises in volume as I focus on the song again. It seems I can focus on one or the other, relegating either song or visual images of words and sentences to the background as I change my focus.

As I watch these words flowing freely around the room, I absorb those I focus on, and as I do, I feel my emotional state fluctuating in sync with the concepts they impart. I feel the weight of these words as they seem to penetrate my soul: "O Lord, make me know my end and what is the measure of my days; let me know how fleeting I am!" This too is part of our human condition, so I allow these wistful feelings to flow through me, giving me longing and desire to be in the King's presence, then realizing and feeling His unseen presence. I try to be silent with my every thought directed to my King, so as not to continue making mistakes before Him. (I have a clear presence of mind, knowing I have made mistakes before others, so I make a mental note to retain this quiet reverence in my future interactions, as I keep on patiently seeking my King for His guidance and deliverance.) My hope is in Him. His Word reminds me life is short, and I am but a shadow. Even though I know one day I will die, I also recognize that dying is the best thing that can happen to me because death has been conquered for those in the King's family. In an instant I will be truly alive in His presence forever. As soon as I come to this realization though, I immediately go back to fretting about how I will deal with my end. I feel my arms rising, and I ask my King to help me face death—to help me be prepared for it.

I begin to think of entering room 40, and as I do, I am suddenly walking through the door. I contemplate how to practice patience through every day my future holds. To emphasize this decision, I sing "As I Wait Upon the Lord." I am also hearing the choir singing the same words. This heady combination brings me to the realization He has heard this and my every cry, He has met my needs, and He has brought me up from the deep pit of mire and mud and, indeed, has put me on a foundation of unshakable rock. He *is* the solid Rock, reminding me of another song about that solid Rock on which I stand. I am rejoicing! He has put a new song in my mouth, as now a third song comes to mind: "Great Things He Has Done."

As I worship my King in this surreal world of purposefully targeted words directed at my spirit, I close my eyes and all the things He has done for me parade before my physically closed but spiritually wide-open eyes. Way beyond just reading and seeing, these words are not only to lodge in my being but to be the basis for understanding and application regarding how I live each moment. I know God has a perfect plan for me and for all those around me. He will indeed continue to meet my needs and rescue me from, or

The King's 19th Palace

through, every difficult turn of (and in) my life. Indeed, instead of destruction, He brings deliverance. The King has saved me, and this is a joyous wonder I *will* proclaim. His love and truth have preserved me, and I see the inadequacy of my own sacrifices, knowing no sacrifice of mine will ever work. I am thankful beyond measure because the King's Son is the once-for-all sacrifice who was perfectly substituted in my place. With my eyes still closed, I think back to the King's First Genesis Palace, room 22, where the King Himself provided the lamb for the sacrifice (and now I am recalling the King's Son as the Lamb in rooms 9 and 10 of the Hebrews Palace). The King has provided for my salvation.

I open my eyes, and when I do, I realize I have been listening to the choir as they sing the essence of this room. Then the visual images of words take precedence again, streaming past then veering suddenly into me as I focus on any particular sentence. Being *struck* by the King's holy Word is a heady experience! Besides my knowing I must apply these truths, I am also to share this knowledge and understanding with others. Testing the parameters of my desire to press into and be pressed by all these many rooms, I close my eyes again and envision room 41. I open my eyes, and directly ahead I am entering room 41, noting an emblazoned label on the door: "The King Is the Preserver of My Life."

I am greeted by a full-throated celestial song: "Blessed is the one who considers the poor!" I am jolted by the volume of the choir, and I realize my exposure to this spirit world has fine-tuned my ability to notice specific patterns dear to the King's heart. I determine to give greater consideration to the poor in my sphere of influence. As I proceed, I note I am on board a large ship with many people in a broad, grand room, filled with exotic hardwood furniture that is silky to my touch. There is not a single object of any kind on the top of any piece of furniture! The exquisitely crafted pieces reflect the King's magnificence, and I marvel at being able to observe and take in some details of the Source of all being.

I know the King will not only preserve me in this life, but He will continue to care for me throughout eternity. Though I may experience great sickness or some other calamity in my sinful life, I gratefully acknowledge the King has given me His salvation, His grace, and His mercy, which have all provided healing for my soul. I know evil will come against me in this life, but I also know the King will ultimately provide justice. He is preparing me and will one day raise me up to dwell with Him forever, so I may always worship my King. I think of how I use my time, talent, and treasure—He has given me all things for life and breath while I dwell here on earth.

I turn to read the words in my line of focus and recognize the last item in this room as a doxology verse of praise, but what grabs my attention is the visual symbol that follows this final verse. I see a bookend that stops before me when the final string of words flows into my being. It hovers before my eyes, as if declaring something. It suddenly strikes me that this bookend signifies the end of the first of the five sections of the rooms in this house. I have just completed my viewing—or hearing with instruction to understand and apply—of the first section of this diverse and amazing 19th Palace. I am immensely thankful for this Guidebook but even more so for the Guide—the true docent—who has led me on this tour of these first 41 rooms. He has led me on a journey of discovery I am hard pressed to describe. I just know I have learned much as I continue to apply this portion of His truth. It is all part of His perfect plan for my life!

Feeling wide awake, I'm keen to explore the next batch of rooms in the second section of the 19th Palace. The bookend hovers before me, and I am suddenly inspired by film scenes I see using modern computer technology to show how a user interacts with holographic images floating before them. I lift my hand and swipe the bookend to my left. A doorway to room 42 appears as I hear the opening verse in song. I can still see the bookend in my peripheral vision, so I reach out and now swipe the bookend to my right. The doorway shrinks as I hear the opening verse of the previous room 41 again. Intrigued by the endless levels of depth and discovery within this magnificent palace, I swipe right again and am stepping into room 42.

It is a large room with two windows, and through the closest window I see an enclosed porch receiving light from a third window. From the words I see floating, I realize the porch is actually room 43, which is attached.

I look out the first then the second window of room 42, and the scene is a group of deer in a field, panting thirstily, and beyond them more deer are making their way down from a far-off mountain. They must, however, travel through a patch of desert to reach the field where the much-needed water is found. Tears fill my eyes as I realize my own throat feels parched and dry. I recognize this feeling—it is because I too feel separated from my King's presence, and I know it is a result of my own wandering through the desert of trivial circumstances that fill our modern life. It is a dry thirst that my tears cannot quench! I move to the second window and see a similar scene, but now I can also see a waterfall with torrents of water cascading down the mountain, and I have a comfortable reminder of the abundant Living Water my King has for me. I feel my spirit drinking in this water, and feeling satisfied, I move to the porch. I see the source of bright light is at the top of the mountain, and it reminds me of the blinding Light that swept through and removed my darkness before being admitted into this Kingdom. I recall how He rescued me and brought me out of the darkness of deceit and depression, which gripped me in a deep funk. I look to the light, and I am no longer downcast. From the depths of my soul, a fountain of thanksgiving erupts for my salvation and for my King!

Filled with joy I see myself crossing the desert easily, then start walking up the mountain toward the bright light. I reach the flat ground at the top, where I walk into a circle of trees. I approach the nearest tree, and as I touch the rough bark, an inscription appears.

Dr. Gene Baillie

My hand merges with the tree, and unlike my previous experiences with portals and doorways, I am suddenly inside a circular room. The wind sighing through the leaves around me echoes the sound of celestial voices breathing their song—the song of the King. I realize I have entered room 44. It is familiar to me, and I know now the light I followed is the light of my King's face, for He delights in me, His servant. I know that every time I enter this room I am encouraged to bring to remembrance the deeds the King performed in the days of my forefathers, in the days of old.

Words are spoken that remind me of their plans and their possession but more importantly of their realization they were unable to save themselves. Instead, the King was behind every detail, even of their own plans. This room brought to my realization the King has always been in charge of everything on this earth, both outside of this Kingdom and inside. This fact explains the many difficulties I encountered while I was yet outside the protective fence, before being given access to the gate of this Kingdom—because those who are not actively *for* the King are sadly *against* Him (as explained by the King's Son in the Matthew Palace, room 12 and item 30). This thought brings me back to the present. I know I cannot trust in my own power to save myself nor indeed for anything else. I understand now I must continually return to this and other similar rooms for encouragement, so as not to deviate from the path the King has set out for me. He knows me through and through to the deepest portion of my heart. He loves me, and always will, so I find myself singing the words to a song that proclaim this truth: "The King's Son loves me, this I know, for His Word tells me so."

All the furniture in this room in the forest is made of surrounding natural materials of rock and wood, including the circular walls. I touch the wall, and the sighing breeze changes inflection as I seem to float seamlessly into room 45. The song of the celestial choir is softer and seems to ebb and flow with the sound of wind in the trees. This room also brings back memories. When I first entered

The King's 19th Palace

the Kingdom, I thought the King was physically present, inhabiting the highest hill. I have subsequently come to realize He is actually ruling from all places at once. I don't understand this completely, but I do know the King is triune in nature, meaning He is Three Persons in One. He is *Father*, enabling me to become an adopted son. He is *Son*, the One who sacrificed for me and led me through the gate. Finally, He is the *Spirit*, the One who transplanted in me my new heart, still another change I certainly feel but do not fully understand.

I reflect upon the Kingdom. Traversing through and learning within all the King's 66 palaces has taught me the Spirit is the One who began this new life in me and gave me the ability to acknowledge the King's Son as Savior. Not only did the King's Son bring me into this Kingdom, He also sacrificed Himself, saving me from my sins and sinful lifestyle, and became Lord of my new life. This is my story, this is my song, my joy, as I praise my Lord all day long. In a spiritual sense (I also perceive Him somehow physically), the King is ever present, here and throughout all of His creation. This particular room describes how the King sent his Son to ride majestically out of His Kingdom to spread His cause of righteousness and truth. I am so grateful to be a part of the army He leads. Now I hear the themes of a teaching poem and a song of true love.

The poem describes how the Son came from His palace to collect His bride and how He takes her to the palace of the King. And attached to the description is a promise this will occur again at a future time. Although the writing suggests a singular, female bride, the closing verse seems to imply *all* adopted children will be the bride. Many other of the King's palaces confirm our relationship to the King as both an adopted child and a bride. All of His adopted children are well prepared for this eventful day: they have received a gift to be truly treasured and have been properly clothed in white—just as a bride *should* be adorned. This is our white robe of righteousness that transforms us and progressively becomes an indwelling and essential part of our very being! We increasingly become a purer white as we draw closer to our Bridegroom.

I touch the wall to exit the room, and the wind in the leaves above this circle of rooms softens then increases gustily as I shift into room 46. I am confronted by a new phenomenon: rooms 47 and 48 are adjoined to the room I stand in, and room 49 extends out to one side. Three somewhat connected circular wooden chambers with the fourth extending to my right.

As I pass through them all, I find the first three somewhat similar, and one central theme is being proclaimed loudly: the King is on *our* side! He provides our safety and is our ultimate defense. Even though everything around us sometimes seems to convey cataclysmic danger—like an earthquake or a mountain falling into the sea that brings with it a huge tsunami—still, we have *nothing* to fear. In the face of such danger we can, in fact, hear the victory horns being blown. At peace, we are able to shout aloud and clap our hands in joyful singing, proclaiming, "Great is the Lord and greatly to be praised" in this city of our great King. As a wave of thoughts and images flows through me, I start singing, "A mighty fortress is our King." Our good God is exalted among the nations, and my song leads me into another melody: "He is a great King over all the earth, clap your hands, all you people, with a voice of triumph." What joy to sing praises to my King! What a privilege to gain this fruitful knowledge, so we can guide coming generations regarding the life-giving truth of our King and His Kingdom. Though I often may be like a docent or guide through the palace, the King is always present and alongside and will guide us *forever*.

I now explore the attached room 49. Added to the soft song of the angelic choir drifting through the leaves above my head is a message printed on the entrance mat: Man in his pomp—yet without understanding—is like the beasts that perish.

I keep my ears open to hear and discern the message carried on the breeze. It speaks of the absolute truth concerning life and death. What I do know is this: though I am a precious, adopted child of the King, I will not live here forever, and no amount of wealth or anything else will be able to ransom me or anyone else. My King gave me the ability to discern this basic truth after I entered into His Kingdom. I know He has ransomed me. I will not have the same end as those who live outside His Kingdom and are not brought in. Whatever wealth or other earthly goods gathered inside or outside this Kingdom, *everything* will be left behind. I can take nothing beyond this life, which makes me so utterly grateful the King has ransomed my soul.

This chapter of my journey has been filled with learning about my King, mostly by absorbing truth both verbal and visual through all my senses into every crevice of my heart and mind—and then being challenged to apply this truth to how I live each moment. I have tried to express in words, but mine lack—so I ask you to pick up your Guidebook and read the account of these and all the rooms in this amazing palace. I am feeling weary. I have experienced so much! I place my palm on the wall's curved surface, and I awake to find I am closing my closet door, with its fresh smell of crisp linen greeting me. Was I sleep-walking or really in the closet! I forego my urge to wake Carol and tell her of my adventure. Tomorrow I will regale her with my journey to the bright Light and the circle of trees.

Chapter 11

The King is the Creator of the universe, our world stage, each of us, and all things. He is the Writer of our script and Director of the playing out of our lives on His provided stage—in every detail. He asks us to learn our lines well from His perfect plan, revealed in His Guidebook. He has spoken and told us what is good—what does He require but to do justice, to love kindness, and to walk humbly with your King (based on Micah 6:8).

"The linen closet? *Our* linen closet?" I can hear the wonder in Carol's voice.

"Yes. *Our* linen closet."

"Wow! That means we can access the King's Palaces from anywhere on earth. We don't have to travel to exotic locations or even a cave in the Appalachian foothills."

"Exactly! It's just as I suspected, and now I know. I think the intention you begin with delivers the required result. Last night my intention was to visit room 39, so that's where I went."

Over breakfast Carol and I discuss the adventure I had while she slept, and after breakfast we agree to visit the King's 19th Palace together—but we decide to focus on the door to our sunroom, just to test the theory that we can access the King's palaces from

The King's 19th Palace

anywhere on earth. We agree to visit room 50 of the palace, and we hold hands as we close our eyes and envision the number 50 on our sunroom door. My eyes are still closed when I hear Carol's gasp. I open my eyes, and the white wooden door to the sunroom has become a natural wooden door that is dark and embellished with intricate carving. The Hebrew symbol representing the number 50 (נ) is glowing on the door.[8]

Carol steps forward and turns the brass handle then steps into the room. I am amazed that she has gained entry without having to open a portal and a doorway. Perhaps I have been complicating the access we are given into the King's Palace. I follow Carol into the room. Again there is a combination of song and strings of visual sentences, which is somehow in my mind when I focus on any single sentence. The song fades into the background as I focus on any visual aspect of meaning contained in this room. We don't need glasses either.

We find ourselves standing before the ultimate Supreme Court of the King. As I fluctuate between focusing on the song of the choir and the words of which this room is comprised, I cannot see, but we both hear the voice of the King speak in favor of His faithful witnesses and the judgments leveled against the wicked. Yet again, I realize how blessed I am to have a covenantal and personal relationship with Him as one of His beloved sons. I have been set free and will glorify my Father the King. Just as I experienced in previous rooms, I see Carol also open herself to the beauty of imbibing God's Word directly into her being. Once we have both absorbed the message contained in this room, we agree to open the door to room 51. As we turn, another door to an adjacent room appears in the wall before us, and as I open the door, I pay attention to the special plaque on the door.

---

8. Hebrew letter for 50 is *nun* also meaning "grace."

The plaque relates to one of the King's princes who committed a great sin (we know it was adultery followed by a cover-up murder of the woman's husband). Although the words we now hear spoken are those of the prince, I immediately know the application—they are a model of how I should respond concerning my own sin—in thought, word, and deed. I have to take my thoughts captive, guard my speech, and always pray before I act. These exercises will enable me to personally experience the grace, love, compassion, and mercy of the King. When He put His Spirit within me and transplanted into me a new heart, He not only gave me the ability to shun the sin-filled life I lived among outside nations and earthly kingdoms, but He also promised to guide and direct my every step as I live in His Kingdom.

As I learned in the Ezekiel Palace in room 36, He not only gave me my new heart within; He also washed away all my sin and gave me a clean record, giving me a desire to follow Him, to read His written words, and to teach other sinners His ways. Just like each of us, however, I am not devoid of sin—my sinful nature persists while I walk the earth. My actual sins are continually exposed before me, yet I continue to rebel against the King and then conceal my sin. I am in constant need of repentance, bringing my sins before the King, asking for the grace of His forgiveness and the covering of His mercy. His Word confirms He is continually making within me a pure heart and a more steadfast spirit, so I can more closely resemble my King with each passing day.

Carol and I agree to visit room 52, and yet again our intention is sufficient to reveal the door to this room. As we enter I receive a profound reminder of how the King transplanted my old nature with a righteous, upgraded version. I must continually resist allowing my old self to regain any foothold in my life.

I go to the balcony, and looking outside, I see a brook lined with trees. A pair of virtual-reality glasses presents itself, and I put them on. The scene becomes scary—one of the trees is being

The King's 19th Palace

uprooted and dragged out of the Kingdom entirely. In its place I see a small olive tree being planted, and as I watch, it begins to grow and flourish. The sequence is repeated, but this time I see a man who is pointing his finger at someone and laughing, then—as if I'm watching a movie—a camera zooms in close, focusing on his tongue. The camera quickly backs away, repeating the entire scene, beginning with the tree being uprooted. This time, however, the man is also swept away. This scene is repeated once more, but this time, as it grows, the small olive tree is transformed into the likeness of my own image. I immediately think of my own tongue and its capacity for deception that causes destruction. I do not want to be swept away! I am remembering room 19 of this palace: "Let the words of my mouth and the meditation of my heart be acceptable in your sight, O LORD, my rock and my redeemer."[9] I thank my King for His guidance and the redeeming changes He has made in me.

I remove my glasses, and as I do, I see Carol removing hers. I want to talk with her later but sense our experience was the same as we exchange a smile—then she nods, and the door to room 53 appears. We step through the door, and immediately we see a side door opening into another room, which I quickly recognize as room 14. It is almost a mirror image to the room we are in. Nearly every word we hear and see reveals the same description. I am reminded—I do not want to be a fool. I know in my heart there definitely *is* a loving God who is my King!

A double door appears before us as soon as we think of moving to the next room, and we both realize we are facing two conjoined rooms—54 and 55. We enter and see projected on the walls old film of the history—outlined and sequentially presented—in both rooms, describing crucial developments within this Kingdom. The same prince who committed adultery in an earlier room is now

---

9. Psalm 19:14

trying to escape the first ruler of a country of the outside kingdom, a king turned evil. The prince is in hiding, but his presence among the local people has been revealed, so he makes his escape to the south. The evil king goes after the prince, but as he is about to surround him, he suddenly retreats, having heard news of an invasion back home by another king. Carol and I listen to the song, and as we see and hear the words of this spellbinding account, we're both glad we are not wearing virtual-reality glasses! The prince asks our King to save him from evil forces, knowing our King is able and willing.

Both of these rooms convey a similar intent, and they teach us about what our King has done for His children in the past, and will continue doing now and in the future to save and preserve those He chooses. Apart from my preservation and application of events such as these, there is another reason for my training in all I am being taught. I know I will be sent out to proclaim the power of my King outside, especially in those places ruled by people with evil intent. I too can ask in prayer. I too will give Him thanks as I continue to trust Him for all aspects of my life and duty. I am the best man for *my part* in His plan. Each of us is being prepared to tell others outside of the Kingdom about our glorious King. Witness this for yourself—put on the virtual-reality glasses, and you, too, will see yourself memorizing lines, moving about, speaking, and acting your part on your stage. You are doing and saying what the Writer and Director of your life-play instructs, while you interact with the people you encounter in all of your acts and scenes. Be sure to go far beyond the words you learn so you can apply them, and then prepare to travel and talk to those who need the King outside of His Kingdom. As we leave, there is a plaque on the wall reading, You cannot feed sheep without food.

I feel Carol's hand on my shoulder, and I sense she is ready to move into room 56. The door again appears and we enter. I put on my glasses and immediately notice a table with an open book and

The King's 19th Palace

a bottle containing clear liquid. I listen to the singing, and as the words are directed into my soul, that's when I realize the bottle contains my tears from the myriad fears and tear-filled miseries I have experienced. I recall and think about the hardships that caused these tears, and when I look at the open book, I see a written record describing these difficult times, which serve to jog my memory. The book has recorded my joyful times, too, as I realize some tears of joy are also mixed in. The King has kept a detailed record of my every moment, including all I have endured, ultimately for my own good and for His glory. He encourages us to sing "When I am Afraid I Will Trust in You," as we praise Him for our safety. I will fear no man because they can only do to me what the King allows. We can confidently ask, "What can man do to me?" These musings bring to mind a life verse I have embraced from the Proverbs Palace: "In his heart or mind man makes his plans or determines his way, but the King guides and directs each step taken."[10] Part of our misery is because of our stumbling as we walk, especially when we are not on the right path! Take courage—though you may stumble, the King will never let you fall to the ground.

I turn to Carol and she smiles. The door to room 57 appears, and by reading the plaque on display, we realize this room is yet another record by the same prince who helped build so many rooms in this 19th Palace. We enter and both express surprise at being in a cave! The choir sings, but instead of sentences floating in the atmosphere, we see writing in light on the dark interior walls. The prince had to run away yet again from the evil king and hid in a cave. We also learn in this darkness he was able to cut off a small piece of the evil king's robe to show him he could have harmed or killed him in this very cave. The writing conveys his post incident reflection on how even outside the Kingdom, the King provided for this refuge until the danger passed. This the King will also do for you and for

---

10. Author's personal translation of Proverbs 16:9

me. We join the words of the prince, singing, "Be exalted, O King, above the heavens, let your glory be known in all the earth."[11]

Our transition into room 58 surprises us both as we finally realize we again *must* touch the wall before a portal then a door appears for us to step through, which we do to continue our explorative journey. We are both shocked at the sudden appearance of three-dimensional creatures, both man and beast—wicked, poisonous, and dangerous creatures, including snakes and lions. There is no singing as we enter, instead an eerie silence. A holographic video clip appears before us, and we see men falling into a river and being washed away. The scene changes to a cooking pot sitting atop a heap of dry thorns, as if ready to cook, followed by a sudden crackling of hot, blazing fire that turns to ash almost instantly. Another scene change reveals a slug sitting near the door being sprinkled with salt. It then disappears, becoming a tiny puddle of water. The sudden sound of rushing wind breaks the silence, blowing away the contents of the entire room. We exchange a "what just happened?" glance. We both perceive this as an example of the King's power, His judgment, and the manner in which He deals with the wicked beyond the Kingdom gate. It is what I might call a "perfect storm."

Much like I imagine wind blowing dust, we are immediately drawn into room 59. Its inscription is "Do Not Destroy." I am spinning, and my mind has swirling thoughts that though we may be threatened with death from various sources, we have the truth and certain hope that even death cannot destroy us. My thinking is that even though that evil king has set a guard to watch over the house in which the prince is hidden—so they can murder him—the prince has seemingly been labeled "Do Not Destroy" by the King. Once again we hear the words about how the King has delivered the prince, met his every need, and provided him with safety and security, out of the reach of these wicked men.

---

11. Psalm 57:5

The King's 19th Palace

As Carol and I find ourselves in a hallway, we continue exploring the 19th Palace. I open the door labeled 60, and I find an armchair to sit in while I listen to the song of the choir. As I sit meditating on the audible and visual words creating this room, I recall the last few rooms we have visited. They all describe the prince's response to one crisis after another. His humanity is reflected in the words, and the record is clear: he does not *always* do the right things. I must, just like him, also trust and depend upon the King. I must remember to rally around His army flag, depend upon His leadership, and follow Him. Not only will He lead me into the battle; He will lead me *through* the battle, to victory.

Too soon we are swept into room 61 and are both immediately struck by the spacious, open-plan design that incorporates two additional rooms, which are separate but accessible. We both join the singing—a loud cry for the Lord to hear our prayers. We are in the midst of a large group, all being reminded the King is our security *in* all things and *from* all things—a tower of strength and a quiet refuge! I find a seat, close my eyes, and quietly sing the song "Take It to the Lord in Prayer." I walk into the attached room 62 and feel led to meditate upon my salvation—my King is my Rock that cannot be shaken. In contrast, I am aware of my own weakness; I am like a leaning wall, a tottering fence, one that is easily shaken and broken down. These words encourage me to trust Him in every circumstance and pour out my heart before Him, and to refrain from speaking falsehood. I am reminded of our goal in life—when judged to have a heart lighter than a feather on the weighing scales. This would have been impossible with my old heart, but now with my new heart, He has made possible what I was incapable of doing on my own.

Into the other smaller room 63 we go, and I am thrilled to see the bright morning light. I open my arms to receive the words of life flowing via the Light throughout this room: our great King is the water my thirsty soul seeks. His strength satisfies my every weakness, for He is mighty and glorious. I feel inspired, and I sing the song "His Love Is Better than Life." As we leave these three rooms, I am excited knowing I will have the opportunity to encourage others to explore this palace as we have, to remember—when sitting in your chair or lying in your bed at night—how much the King has been a help to you. You are protected in the shadow of His wings.

I see a pair of virtual-reality glasses on a table as we enter room 64 and I put them on. I find myself in a hiding place, a refuge provided by the King. I can see everything, but He shields me against the onslaught of arrows of every evil zinging close. The room is decorated with arrows and bows, slings and swords. I see the wagging tongues of evildoers, their verbal onslaught a piercing mental attack against the good guys. As the wickedness of these yammering tongues unfolds before my eyes, they stimulate memories of me having to endure verbal attacks, as well as my own verbal attacks against others. Enduring the wicked words of evil people is akin to the onslaught of slings and arrows, like a sword thrust deeply into your being and viciously twisted. After a brief calm, I am spotted, and more wicked words are now leveled against me in an attempted ambush. Then, however, I see the Words of the King marching to my defense. As the enemy's words attack me on flighted arrows, the King's Word easily deflects them, and they are boomeranged back upon the evildoers who started the attack. I gladly remove the glasses, and we exit the room.

The glass sliding doors of room 65 are open, and we are greeted by an expansive view of the countryside from the deck. As we again put on glasses, I am reminded our King is way more than just a hiding place. Carol and I immediately break out in a spontaneous prayer of praise because with every glance, in all directions, we see images of ourselves everywhere we look and sense the unseen presence of the King. He is ever-present, keeping us from serious rebellion, providing us a dwelling place, providing stability, and ordering all things. We view the mountains and the sea, knowing they are but two magnificent examples of His ordered creation. My eyes linger on a sweet and special rural scene—a countryside of crops and animals, appearing as though the meadows have clothed themselves with flocks of sheep, and the valleys have decked themselves with grain. Carol is also drinking in this scene, her eyes bright with the joy and wonder our great King inspires. All of creation, including my gorgeous wife and I, are clothing ourselves with His bounty to present ourselves to the King. Wherever my gaze falls, I see abundant joy, including my own. We praise the King for His goodness, for His salvation, and for our ability to trust in Him for all things. I joyfully present myself to Him.

Chapter 12

Every second counts! And our King is sovereign over absolutely every moment and detail of our lives. Every footprint we leave on sand or land, even though quickly unseen to man, remains.

I feel a squeeze on my hand. We are back—or did we ever leave our sunroom? Only two hours have passed! I am relieved because I had forgotten about an appointment with our insurance agent. We still have an hour, so Carol drives while I read through some policy changes we hope to make.

We arrive at the office building and enter the elevator. Just as the doors are closing, a young couple arrives, breathless, and running fast toward the elevator doors. I press the button to prevent the doors from closing, and the couple gratefully join us.

"Thank you, Sir. We're late for an appointment."

"My pleasure, glad we can help. My name is Gene, and this is Carol," as I note they have taken places opposite one another.

They are going to the fourth floor too. The doors close and we start rising. Just past the second floor, however, the elevator jerks to a sudden halt. The young man gasps, and I note the sweat on his forehead. "Of all the days this could happen!" he exclaims. The young woman looks at him with a placative gesture.

I know God has a purpose in all things, and I feel this might be part of the Lord's plan for us to further explore. First, though, I must put the couple at ease, and the only thing that comes to mind is to make a suggestion: "Let's pray—I believe God will give us some options."

Glancing both ways, I see a look of interest in their eyes. He nods vigorously, clearly desperate for some intervention to help solve this problem. "What options? Indeed, let's pray!"

Not wanting to complicate matters, I turn to the elevator doors and place a palm on each door. I close my eyes as I first feel the familiar vibration followed by heat. The inscription 66 appears between my hands. They are both spellbound as the elevator doors open to darkness. I see, rather faintly, a table with four pairs of glasses. We reach for them, and as we put them on, we realize they are night-vision goggles—and we step out into room 66. "Don't worry, we've done this before." Carol gently ushers them through the door.

As we hear the opening verse in song, I can't help smiling at the dazed wonder on the faces of our new guests: "Shout for joy to God, all the earth; sing the glory of his name; give to him glorious praise!" I am sure they thought we had only gotten them off the elevator to find a stairway, hearing music from a speaker system. There are no visuals accompanying the song, and I wonder if this is because our newcomers have limited experience or because we have accessed the palace in this novel manner. We see the room is furnished with mahogany and oak, and the velvet drapes are royal purple. Carol engages our newcomers in conversation, and I leave her to take them on a tour of the room, one I am sure they think is a sitting area for the offices of that floor. I sit in a large leather armchair, and I close my eyes as I listen to the words, "You have tested us . . . You have laid a crushing burden on our backs . . . we went through fire and through water; yet You have brought us out to a place of abundance."

Dr. Gene Baillie

Since Carol and I have started seeing the King as our Provider of all things, including this new place, we have begun to recognize our duty to share the King's truths with others. Indeed, we have been given this particular opportunity as part of His perfect plan. Because we have learned to trust in Him completely, we are more easily able to see we are being trained to glorify Him by telling others about Him. They can only hear and perceive if and as the King gives them the ability, but *we* have the responsibility, as His adopted children, to truthfully portray all He has done. Carol and the young couple see examples of His goodness and deliverance all around this room, confirmed by the words of its song. On the walls appear vibrant, moving images of His creation, all of His works, and His incomparable strength in all circumstances.

I watch them for a moment as they soak up the song and Carol's words, spellbound as she recounts how He has brought both her and I through every trial or adversity. She speaks of how we praise Him for refining us through fire and cleansing us with water as the song and images echo her refrain. Honor and trust are due Him for all the marvelous things He has done for our very souls. Carol encourages them both to sit with us for a while and pray, assuring them He will reveal the truths they need.

We rise and immediately are in room 67. We are all struck by blessings falling upon our upturned faces like a torrential rainfall, demonstrating the goodness and provision of our King. After the shower of blessings, bright rays follow the downpour as if the face of our King is shining upon us. Then our ears hear singing about how gracious He is and how He showers blessings upon us. It blesses me greatly knowing His guidance is not for me alone, but that I can also be a blessing. I watch as the couple seem to talk to one another or give Him thanks, and then I join them, aware as we see expanding circles of people all showing His grace extending to include all the outside nations who have yet to experience His goodness. Our new friends ask for more detail about the manner

The King's 19th Palace

in which all this is happening, and how we are able to access the palace. Carol updates them on our many adventures in this realm, and I open the door to room 68.

As I walk in, we change to provided virtual-reality glasses. The young man emits a low whistle as he puts them on. Outside the walls we all witness a swarm of enemies scattering then vanish—as smoke disappearing into thin air, then candle wax melting and disappearing before its advancing flame. I then realize the King's highway is being built. Then an army is on the mountains with chariots swooping in to save a host of captives, bringing them back from the brink of death. Even the regiment with the least men is now dominant as they fall in with the victorious, returning army. Just as I was given the ability to hear truth then instructed by others who already knew the way, I too was once brought across the divide from that evil place of slavery by way of the King's highway into this glorious Kingdom. And now as a servant who truly prospers, I have learned firsthand the difference between a slave and an obedient and willing servant.

Now it is time to carry out His marching orders. I am finding my place in the ranks, joining the army of the King. I too will travel outside of the Kingdom to make His name known throughout all the kingdoms beyond. I will show others the King's highway, which is the way of salvation, possible only through the King's Son. What a joy it is to comprehend my blessings and privileges, and to bless my King in turn by being a blessing to others—like this young couple we have befriended. They too once knew the King more closely but have wandered far from His Kingdom. Before arriving at the elevator, they were caught in a difficult and personal situation. How graciously our King responds to every request, and we know His timing is perfect as we rejoice when we see answers we desire. We remove our glasses, and the young man says, "Gene, Carol, thank you for sharing the King's Palace with us. We know and feel His presence, and I know in my heart He is guiding all of us." The young lady agrees enthusiastically, "This is no accident—God directed the details of our elevator meeting down to mere seconds!" As Carol opens the door into room 69, and before we cross the threshold, Carol relates some important information about this room, having personally studied it in great detail.

"This is a very different room—one which addresses our concerns as the King's children—regarding those times when we are assigned to go outside the gates into surrounding kingdoms that are steeped in evil and so many other worldly temptations. I think all of us, when we first came here, thought we would continually reside within these gates, secure within the Kingdom walls . . . and in a sense we do. At some point though, we realize it is our privilege to go beyond the walls into outside kingdoms. At first this can be quite disturbing. Remember, we all used to dwell outside. We have been changed, but we know this was not for our benefit alone. We have not only learned, but we have been trained. We are being trained daily and will continue to learn more every day concerning the message and promises of the King."

Carol pauses momentarily then turns to face the young couple. "You will both indeed need to learn and apply more and more of the King's truth to your directed path, and we will pray you will both be zealous in sharing everything that takes place in this Kingdom, including every advantage we all enjoy. Still, remember this: your message will fall on deaf ears, except for those whose hearts are opened by the King—those whom the King has granted the ability to hear His Word and to perceive His truth. You will encounter and interact with people living outside this Kingdom who disagree with you, sometimes violently. At other times people will listen to you politely as you tell them about this Kingdom and its King. Some will pity you for expressing your thoughts and comments, and still others will ask you to join them in their evil thoughts, words, and

The King's 19th Palace

deeds as they encourage you to forsake the King for moments of earthly pleasure." The young lady glances at her husband with a smile, and he nods knowingly, smiling back.

We see four pairs of glasses in room 69, so we put them on. I find myself in a compelling situation, desperately needing to cross a body of water. On my first attempt, I step off the bank, but I sink immediately into a deep hole with water up to my neck. Flailing wildly, I cry out for help, but there is no one there to save me. I turn and make my way back to the bank then try again a few paces to the right, quickly realizing it is becoming progressively muddier with each step. The water resembles a marshy bog with thick mud that acts like quicksand! There is nowhere to step without sinking deeper into the now smelly mire. Just as I am about to head to the bank, I suddenly feel firm footing again, but before I can heave a sigh of relief, I see an overwhelming body of floodwater heading toward me. Now, everywhere I turn there is deep water . . . I am close to panicking, and I feel as though I will soon drown. In my mind I recall from the Isaiah Palace, "When you pass through the waters, I will be with you . . . they shall not overwhelm you."[12]

I continue crying out to be saved, but there is no one to be seen and my throat is parched, my voice hoarse. I cannot drink this dirty water. Then, suddenly, the scene changes. I realize I am stepping into the midst of a crowd who are listening to me only to confront my words. I sense they are intent on confusing and challenging everything I say. Wherever my thoughts turn, I still can't escape the sense of sinking into a deep hole. As I turn, another group confronts my words. Again, I feel I am sinking into the boggy mire of all the evil words they are spewing at me. What do I say next? I don't know how to confront their vitriol. I feel overwhelmed and exasperated.

Panic stricken, I rip off my glasses, and immediately I realize the words of this room are proclaiming a vital message:

---

12. Isaiah 43:2

> This is the acceptable season to learn about the King—to *know* His committed love and leading and the truth of His salvation. He will deliver you from the mire and mud; He will lift you up and not let you sink. He will not let you fail, even from deep within the depths that seem to overwhelm you. The mire and quicksand along the edges will not close in over you.

I remember my former rebellious life, knowing it was a dishonor to my King. I remember the wickedness of my ways. I know that some outside the Kingdom—but not all—are at this point in time just as I once was. Some among them are chosen—those who will respond to the message and will seek to follow the King. Those who will be changed will be allowed to enter into the Kingdom to dwell forever. Or I should say, the King will have His Spirit change their hearts, then they, too, will have the ability to hear and respond *then* be led into the Kingdom to dwell. The young couple have also removed their glasses and are both crying, clinging to one another and praising the King for rescuing them from their wandering. It has been a heart-wrenching lesson, so I suggest we sing a song of praise together: "Love Lifted Me." On the Lord my solid Rock I stand, all other ground is stinking, shifting, sinking sand.

Our new friends have regained their composure as I open the door to room 70. As we walk into this room, we hear the choir reminding us of the help we all so desperately desired from the King in our times of need. Before exiting the room, we discuss how each one of us wanted His help to arrive sooner, yet we all recognize a simple truth: our King always comes to help us at exactly the right time. Carol suggests to the young woman she should open the door to room 71, and she does with the glee of a child picking flowers on a spring morning. Both she and the young man seem thrilled at the King's timely intervention on this critical day of their lives.

The King's 19th Palace

The verse of song in this room reminds us yet again of everything the King has done for us, and to request His continued blessings. The song tells how wonderfully our King cares for us. Though we may think He began His care for us once we entered into His Kingdom, we are mistaken. He's been the one we have trusted unknowingly since our youth, and in fact, He has been in charge of every aspect of our lives even prior to our birth, and from the moment of our conception onward! Each of us continues to witness a personal video recounting and reviewing our life. We see He has always been our hope, our strength, our provision, our protection, our salvation, our Teacher. Though it is said a picture is worth a thousand words (and this video even much more), nothing is sufficient to describe everything He has done for me. Even over a lifetime I would be unable to make a complete list of what He has done for my well-being. All I can do is stand in this room to thank and praise Him, as I start singing, "Great is the King and greatly to be praised!" Carol and the young couple join me in song, and our hearts are so filled with joy as we sing another song: "He's Got the Whole World in His Hands."

The young man is eager to open the door to room 72, and when we follow him, we see projected onto the walls a detailed listing of our King's judgment and granted righteousness continued, which we see He is passing on *in and through* his Son. The greatness of our King is once again revealed, emphasizing everything we learned in the last room. The celestial choir is singing about how our King has dominion over absolutely everything and every detail throughout the universe. He also provides for every human need, including judgment and food, and is a shield of protection over the weak and oppressed. Innumerable are the blessings provided by our King! "Blessed be his glorious name forever; may the whole earth be filled with his glory!"

We enter room 73, a room I love. I am surprised to see no sign of a bookend because I know this room depicts the start of the third section of rooms within the 19th Palace. But we do see an amazing hologram with two questions about the King, and one question about His children, each followed by its answer. First, "Is the King good?"

"Yes! He is *always* good in every aspect, especially to those who are His children, for they have received a new, changed heart." The King is good and does good.

Second question: "Does the King know all things?"

"Yes. The King is all-knowing and omniscient—He knows absolutely everything, and He is ever-present, everywhere, at all times."

Then a question about you and I as His children: "If I walk astray from His path, do I have any hope?"

"Yes, our King is the God of hope! He has a perfect plan and is the Fountain of all knowledge. He is the Writer and Director of your life and how it plays out, from start to finish. If you are His child, you will enjoy a future of glory with your King forever in His dwelling place. Every step you take—even footsteps on the sand of the seashore—though they seem to be washed away by the next high tide, each step still had a purpose and is actually still there, though they are no longer discernible to us." The answer to this question strikes a chord within the young couple, and they are greatly encouraged by the message contained within this room.

The young lady tells us she and her husband have recently strayed into dark outer kingdoms even though they know the King. This led to a downturn in their marriage with separation from God and one another. They relate that respect and love roles have been reversed. When we met them in the elevator, they were on their way to see an attorney to begin divorce proceedings. The man feels confident even their absence of prayer has been confronted with an answer. Though there will certainly be consequences, the King is in the process of rescuing them. We all agree that as you follow the King and His Son, you are essentially following in Their footsteps mentally and physically, though you do not see them.

We have all absorbed the necessary information stored in this room, so we go on to room 74. Having spent time in this room and the next, I suggest to my companions we first visit the attached room 75 so we can see the end result of what is described in room 74. We join the choir in giving thanks to the King for all the wonderful things He has done, then we hear a recounting of His wondrous deeds. No images or holograms, no glasses, just words to hear and digest. We gain a clear understanding of how He has been governing and judging the outside kingdoms—it is God alone who executes judgment. He has been our example, and He has taught us continually, all in His perfect timing. Having gained this clarity, we now go back to room 74.

Yet again the King's Word reinforces and reviews the concept that when we are assigned to the outside kingdoms, we may well wonder where the King is and how His promises can possibly be obtained and delivered, and it is reiterated that almost everyone will be opposed to us and our message. We perceive our warrior status, knowing we may be harmed and possibly even suffer as we carry out His perfect plan for our lives. We are reminded of how He will use us, and how we will serve Him. We will surely also have feelings of depression and failure, but at these junctures, it is crucial for us to remember all we have been taught, so we can bear in mind these feelings are enemies of the King. Then a presentation begins on the far wall as we hear and see an example of our being made into a polished and straight arrow. First, a portion of tree is selected, the bark removed, and a knot-free part is then slowly kiln dried. Then the carving begins, followed by polishing. Finally, an arrowhead is attached with a notch at the opposite end. Just as He stores you as a carefully crafted arrow, He may keep you safely in His quiver for shorter or longer periods, to use you in peaceful scenarios or in places of raging battle, all as He alone desires. He will defend His cause through you, and He will win.

I see another door, and thinking it is the entrance to room 76, I open it. My companions follow me in, but when the door closes, we are back in the elevator, which is now working and on its way to the fourth floor. Carol and I embrace our new friends as we stand in the corridor, knowing just as we have, they too have been blessed by their encounter with the King's 19th Palace. We exchange phone numbers and agree to stay in touch and pray for one another. What a blessing it is to serve our great King, knowing we have been an instrument in the hands of the Lord to help this couple regain their trust in our almighty King to redirect their lives.

Chapter 13

Be a straight arrow for the King as you walk in His Light!

Carol wakes me and hands to me a cup of tea. We say our morning prayers, and I reach for my Bible, turning to the Psalms, but Carol puts her hand on my leg. "Let's spend time exploring this wing of the Psalms Palace in person. Let's try the linen closet—I haven't entered the palace through that door yet." She smiles sweetly, knowing I can't resist the offer of an adventure.

I walk across to the door and close my eyes to visualize the next room number. I open my eyes and turn the brass handle that has appeared. Carol takes my hand and we enter, revealing the opulence of rooms 76 and 77. We hear the melodic words of each room as we roam between the two, and we are once again able to see streams of words also drifting through the rooms, veering directly toward us as we focus on specific words. After comprehending the context of the first room, Carol starts singing the song "My King Reigns," so I join her in song, marveling at how appropriate it is within the landscape of these rooms. We are clearly able to see the dynamic power the King has in His revealed Word. What He speaks becomes law, and what He speaks is being done immediately, without question! His enemies will stand before Him judged, just as His Word proclaims.

The King's 19th Palace

We of this Kingdom are sometimes afraid our King is not listening and won't come to help us. In these moments, when we feel exhausted and deprived of sleep, just remembering our King's love and His promises keeps our eyes open. The enemy will not win. The King's army will come, and we can depend upon His strong, right hand. I go back into room 77, and on a carved wooden table, I pick up the virtual-reality glasses. I put them on, immediately seeing the King's prevailing wonders and His unmatched strength—enemy arrows are flying in every direction, seemingly in the midst of a whirlwind, even as lightning flashes and thunder booms throughout the landscape. I witness roaring seas carrying the King's enemies away in a torrential flood. As the amazing battle ceases and victory is declared, I see long-dead patriarchs leading sheep through His Kingdom gates. I remove my glasses, realizing I am still marching, my mind marveling at my King and knowing I can trust Him completely. Why should I ever doubt? It is just a matter of simple faith and certain hope. I turn to look for Carol and see she is holding a door open.

I love this large, double-vaulted space in room 78! As you—reading this account—explore with me, I encourage you in your mind's eye to look around and marvel as you absorb its teaching, as you give ear to its words describing all our ancestors. It speaks of their many trials, how they failed and did not follow the proper way at all times, how they persevered, how they came back to depend upon, trust, and obey their King—how they saw no other path but to trust and obey. This room truly inspires me to sing some words of "Trust and Obey," for there really is no other way. Carol hands me glasses and I them put on. At first it seems as if there is a rock concert being observed in the desert. I see a lot going on, but I pay attention to the area where throngs are shouting and complaining they have run out of water. They obstinately declare they will die of thirst in this dry and miserable desert. I notice the leader takes a rod in his hand that projects surreal images in the sky—I see this rod is being used to strike the Egyptians with plagues.

The boisterous crowd immediately quiets as they do not want to be struck down. Instead, the rod is used to strike the Rock, and suddenly there is water gushing forth from the Rock, forming streams and huge rivers. Then appears a cross in the place of the rock with a human likeness hanging—suspended between heaven and earth—and being struck. Words spoken are heard, "Come to me all who are thirsty, and I will give Living Water springing up to eternal life." These words bring to remembrance other information about Living Water in four more of the King's palaces: "Exodus," room 17; in the first palace built for the Corinthian Church, room 10; in the palace built upon the words of the apostle John, rooms 4 and 7; and finally in the Palace of Revelation, room 22. I am now feeling hunger and thirst, recognizing that within the Kingdom borders all my needs are met abundantly.

We open another door, but it leads into a hallway with many open doors leading off to the left and right. We see a large bronze plaque on the wall, so we stop to read it:

> As you visit the next eleven rooms (79 to 89), each will vary in its teaching and learning experience and will also present a history lesson. Focus on viewing each room from these three vantage points: our ancestors, the King, and your own trials. These lessons are very important as you continue to prepare for your assignment in the outside kingdoms. In order to keep your attention, in each room you will be presented with what seems to be a haphazard mixture of questions and situations. In the end, all is designed to keep you focused, to stimulate your thoughts, and to help your recall in upcoming interactions.

The King's 19th Palace

We then read the next, larger plaque that clearly explains part of the reason for studying these rooms:

> The rooms are designed to prepare you for the variable and sometimes surprising onslaught you will face each time you are outside the protective fencing of this Kingdom. As you visit each room, you will have many of the same feelings, disappointments, opinions, and reactions as those who walked before us. You will often notice a collage of pictures on the walls (even some with a 3D effect), see objects in the rooms, and at certain times, you will be able to visualize past interactions with the enemy, recorded for your benefit. Sometimes you will hear people talking or the wind blowing or experience unusual visual effects. You will see how those before us sometimes wondered if the King was near or present at all, while at other times they are gladly praising Him for His rescue and for fighting their battles. Learn much from this multiple-format teaching process. As you walk through each of these rooms, certain highlights will be brought to your attention. You will be experiencing a multimedia presentation and will recognize when to use your virtual-reality glasses—or sometimes those for night vision.

Carol and I exchange a glance. She reaches for my hand, and we enter room 79. As I look around, I realize we both are now outside the walls of the King's domain. We listen to the song of this room and watch the visual display of sentences depicting the room's essence. We talk in hushed tones, discussing how our forefathers shed their own blood trying to preserve their inheritance in the outside kingdoms, and even struggling to save the place of worship dedicated to their King. As they lost some of the battles, the surrounding peoples had the audacity to ask them, "Where is your King?" The King, however, has a perfect and continuing plan, as well as a promise that includes—surprisingly—the seemingly failed thoughts, words, and deeds we all experience as Kingdom people. It brings me great relief to remember the King's plan includes you and I, who are both being prepared for our assignments on the outside, where we will carry out our tasks as part of His mighty army.

We move to room 80, which has lots of visual stimuli. We see a picture on the wall, an unusual hologram of our forefathers eating bread made of tears, and viewed at a slightly different angle, we see them drinking those same tears. The song we hear encourages us—even though those before us experienced the sorrow of tears, they will see the King's Light of salvation shine over them yet again. On another wall we see a 3D movie of a vine that was transplanted from another nation. It was put down, took root, and now covers the land. Then the plant transitions into trees and becomes a forest, advancing and replacing the existing forest we see being cut and burned down in front of the advance. I commit this image to memory, recalling the recommendation given in the bronze plaque to "Learn much from this . . . teaching process." The scene is a reflection of how our King of Light is sweeping over the land while our battle rages in the outer realms. It is a reminder for us to be light to the populace about who the King is and how He leads while we participate in the raging battle!

We enter the next door along the hallway, room 81. Immediately we are swept up by a crowd of people, surrounded by music, song, and dance. We walk with the crowd, but it's difficult to find our way in the almost total darkness. I take Carol's hand. We hear people speaking foreign languages that we struggle to translate, and we see them beckoning us to enter into their festival tents. Suddenly we hear our own language, and our gaze falls upon a tent of light displaying the banner of our King. We quickly join the crowd thronging this tent, joyfully waving and beckoning for more people to come through the gate into our chosen tent. We look around and realize the people in this tent are serving special living water, along with bread and honey.

Some join us, but sadly, many people favor the darkness of the beckoning pleasures of surrounding tents, rather than walking into the bright-light tent. We join our brethren in singing as we beckon to the passing crowd, "You have been affected by the fall; if you tarry, you will never come at all." We pray for those seeking what appears to be fun and enjoyment in the dark, outer realms—those who, often unwittingly, stumble and prefer this deception to the Light that fills our tent. When we talk about people being hell-bent, it means hell and eternal separation from the King and is the destination they face. Many houses are in that outer darkness, and though they may seem quite enticing, in truth they are deceitful, dead, haunted houses filled with stench. Their only light is a consuming fire. I know this, for I was on that path until the King changed my heart and I followed His Son through the Kingdom gates.

Carol finds a side door that opens to room 82, and as we enter, we see it is a spacious courtroom that sits directly and precisely upon the line dividing the bright light from the extreme darkness we just experienced. We see our King upon the judgment seat, which also is a throne. We see people being led out of the darkness into the presence of the King. We celebrate when they join us, but it is heart-wrenching to see others being cast out. They cross the dividing line, walk into the outer darkness, and disappear. With racing hearts we quickly exit the room and stand for a moment in the hallway, catching our breath before entering room 83.

Upon entering room 83, we find two pairs of glasses, but when we put them on, we quickly realize they are night-vision glasses—as if the courtroom scene was not enough, we now have the ability to see into that outermost darkness. We see people and their leaders gathering, combining their kingdoms to ensure our Kingdom of light is surrounded by evil. They are plotting together to take over the Kingdom of our King. We suddenly hear wind, and then we see a maelstrom of fine dust, chaff, and tumbleweed swirling in front of us. We watch as the cloud of debris disappears, seemingly consumed into a background of fire. I look to the left and see this fire is also burning a forest, permitting us sufficient light to see the mountains in the background, also ablaze with an all-consuming fire. The focus of our glasses is suddenly magnified, zooming in to reveal a frightening truth: all of the "chaff" and "trees" are actually people. Carol and I are both overwhelmed with sadness for all those people who entered the wrong tents. This terrifying appearance is like Mount Doom and yet another reminder of what it means to be eternally isolated from the King.

Shaken, we take a moment to compose ourselves out in the hallway before entering room 84. What a contrast we have in this bright room! The sun is shining, glinting off the King's shields stored all around, just as I remember in room 3. We sit a short while, praying and catching our breath. We have come to realize dwelling with our King is not only what we greatly desire, but it has become our reality, giving us much joy. We spontaneously sing, "A day in the house of the King is better than a thousand elsewhere." We are constantly being prepared to speak about our King in the outer realms, so we thank Him for this teaching and for giving us a portion of His strength to persevere, plus the knowledge of what to say. He is like the sun with its light and warmth and like a shield, which is our strength and protection. Fear and faith both involve taking steps into realms we cannot see or know. We *will* take these faith steps! We *will* go forward in the faith and the strength, which is seemingly our own, but both are really from Him. I'm so thankful for the training I have received, giving me the ability to share the reason for this certain hope within me.

Filled with vigor, we continue into room 85, which at a glance displays more of the history of our forefathers. Generation after generation did not follow the King and were flippant concerning their sin. Time and again they said they would obey but then turned and disobeyed according to their own desire. We look more closely, noticing two groups of people in this room: those who look terrified and those who are filled with awe. What a good lesson concerning the dual aspects of fear! I need those times of awe.

To the side of the room, we behold an amazing sight. Banners seem to be sprouting from the ground. Each banner develops, grows, and disappears, leaving a word in its wake that grows continually larger—until we can read them easily, as new ones repeatedly sprout over and over again. First, we see the words *Love* and *Truth*, which intermingle and touch one another, followed by banners displaying *Righteousness* and *Peace*. The banner for righteousness does not disappear but hangs in the air above the landscape. As we gaze upward, we see this banner descend and begin to surround and "clothe" those filled with awe, who then in faith proceed, following the banner leading them along the King's highway. They are properly clothed for battle and are granted every necessary provision. I am overwhelmed with the feeling of a consistent and unchangeable King who is teaching, guiding, preparing, and then leading even us into battle. We, too, will help plant His banners in victory! We leave the room feeling greatly revived, rejoicing and looking forward to enjoying His peace.

Entering room 86, we immediately realize there is another lesson to be learned: the King continues to hear our prayers. He saves us and keeps us, all due to His grace and mercy in granting us the honor of being His beloved children. We also know He is good, all-forgiving, and the One who loves us. These things are excellent to dwell upon in prayer, which we do for a few minutes, as we perceive and acknowledge He is King among all the kings. We also recognize the things we have repeatedly learned in these rooms are only a small portion of what He does for us, our all-sufficient One! May we reflect His glory as others see Him through our sharing and example. We sing, "King of kings, and Lord of lords" before exiting the room.

We enter room 87, and in the distance my glasses reveal the King's mountain, an eternal dwelling place, even though I was not here when the foundation of this Kingdom and its mountain were laid. After being reborn and receiving my new heart, I can now call this Kingdom the place of my birth and eternal dwelling. My name is recorded in the book of life. I marvel at this blessing I have received, so before we leave the room, we sing two songs: "How Firm a Foundation" and "Rock of Ages."

In room 88, continuing to wear our virtual-reality glasses, a great sadness comes over me when I observe a multitude of hopeless, lost, and wandering people. I flinch when I see the evil they are doing. Their facial expressions illustrate the tremendous depravity of people doomed to a life in that utter darkness of the outside kingdoms. The evil they perpetrate leads them to increasingly feel the loss and hopelessness of having no one to trust—it exacerbates their feeling of imprisonment. This is a sad room, filled with doom and gloom. "I want to get out of here!" I mutter under my breath. This room reminds me of where I used to live.

I feel Carol's hand on my arm, realizing she has heard me. "Sure, Gene. We can leave, but let's use this experience as a reminder of the King's desire for us to learn well His truth and the principles He has given us, so we can share them with those living in fear." We both sit and quietly share the godly heritage in both of our families, the specific spouse we now know is eternally in the King's presence, and the influence we have on one another, our families, and all those the King has us in training to interact with and share His truth. I put my hand over hers, filled with gratitude for this godly woman my King has blessed me with.

Back in the hallway, we face the last of the eleven rooms referenced in the bronze plaque: room 89. What a relief it is to enter this room! Greater than a thousand combined fireworks displays, a continuous light and sound show reveals all the expressions of the King's love, and in such a multitude of ways. His love establishes faithfulness. He loves His chosen ones. He shows His love through His creation and His provision. His committed love results in righteous judgment. His love is expressed in beauty, favor, and strength. I'm thankful to be so dearly loved. His love means He is faithful to His covenant promises and He will not change. I open my arms as I am filled with the essence of this room through hearing the choral verses and through focusing my eyes on each word and sentence as it scrolls.

Having gleaned the wisdom of these past eleven rooms, I recognize how important it is to teach these same truths inside and also on the outside: how people should not reject the King, and how they should neither exclusively think about nor perform their own desires, for absent following the King, such thoughts and acts ultimately lead to those realms of eternal darkness. I also need to explain to people why they should not try to break through the wall into this Kingdom on their own. The only path to entry is through the King's Son.

We need to focus on helping them to acknowledge their sin and then ask the King to save them. As we sit and contemplate our visit in this last of this set of rooms, we realize we have been given a "show" that we might "tell" of our own journey and spiritual situation. We sit in plush crimson armchairs and talk about the pinpoint-accurate "teaching" of these rooms—truly the "show and tell"—and how it has inspired us to grapple with the "learning" required of us. We know we will be "tested" as well. Holding hands in our comfy chairs, we sing, "The King so loved us He gave us His only Son." We enjoy the holy peace that settles upon us, and we sing another song that captures this moment succinctly: "I am no longer a slave to fear, but I am a child of the King."

Chapter 14

My King, please continue to reveal to me in every way in every day Your guiding in and through each step of my life journey—all is beautiful and in Your time.

It's a hot, glorious day, and Carol and I are in Nebraska. I'm showing her the farm that has been in my family since homesteaded in the 1800s. I see the slightly raised area in the grassy field near the site of the now-absent home I have childhood memories of, playing in the nearby creek, catching tadpoles. As I see the earthen raised mound with an old and decaying wooden door, I remember going down the few cement steps into the small cavelike cellar each spring, clearing out sprouting potatoes, pumpkin, and soft squash still stored in this root cellar. I would help collect baskets of items then dust the shelves and sweep the floor in preparation to receive the new summer's crops. I also planted potatoes, cutting a portion with the "eye" and its sprout. I don't know what to expect as I pull upward on the handle to lift the door. Pushing back lots of cobwebs, we gingerly take a step down. Suddenly, we are tumbling downward. We find ourselves in a cool, quiet place, realizing it is the 90th room of the palace. Not the old veggies, spiders, or the dusty and musty atmosphere I expected!

The room is large and sparsely furnished, but all around is a wide variety of clocks and hourglasses on shelves and on the floor,

The King's 19th Palace

each in some way a reminder of how we move through our earthly seasons—which is pertinent, given our age with the many changes of seasons we have been through and are currently experiencing. It has been a few days since we visited the previous eleven rooms. We learned so much on our last excursion, so we decided to take some *time* to process the knowledge gained. With so much more to see and learn, we must also wisely use our *time* exploring this room. After a *season* to reflect and remember, a panorama opens up before us, revealing a multitude of shifting time sequences displayed across the landscape.

As these cycles of time repeatedly shift through their seasons, a man appears—then many humans, sprouting up from the ground then disappearing as they return to the ground. In the background as each created person appears, we notice how each of them then seems superimposed onto one of the green leaves of a tree. Each leaf is at first green, only to turn varying shades of red, yellow, and brown before the combined, layered image falls to the ground to decay and become dirt again. The scene changes, and we are suddenly confronted with a mirror image of ourselves. We are glowing in the dark, and as we watch, we realize the glow is pulsing like a heartbeat to reveal the various deeds of our past. We hear the words we speak—sometimes coarse—and we become aware of our previous thoughts, now flowing before our mind's eye! Then we see our open chests, each undergoing the process of having a beating heart placed within. We each see our own image displayed on a leaf of the tree. At first we grow then we age, dropping to the ground to decay, then we flow to the roots of the tree.

The scene shifts again, returning to the collective groups of people being superimposed onto the green leaves of a tree that include our own ancestors and our offspring. Only now, numbers are being superimposed onto each image, indicating a flurry of days then years—each one progressing until it reaches a count of 70 and sometimes even 80. Like birds they are flying quickly by, as each one disappears and each leaf returns to dirt, becoming fertilizer for the next season of leaves. The scene again shifts suddenly, reflecting a change to seconds, and I realize in just my own cycle of life, more than two-and-one-half billion seconds have flown by! A message appears beneath the large, green tree: "Number your days by years or seconds, however you wish, but gather a heart of wisdom for your walk."

I read a second message that has appeared: "Each second is counted and counts!" Again, Carol and I each see an image of ourselves. We are waking up in the morning, then traveling beyond the gates of the Kingdom, speaking and sometimes engaged in conversation passionately to all who will listen. We watch, transfixed as we go about showing and telling whoever will hear all the wonderful things the King has done for us during the *time* He has granted us. Are we ready? Not completely. Are we prepared? Not perfectly—but we are a work in progress, and we must depend on our King to establish the work of our hands, our voices, and our minds as we pursue His Kingdom work in the outside world.

Let's pause a moment to consider exactly what that work is. As we have explored the rooms of the King's Palaces, each of us has been prepared in the same way with the same instruction, but the pattern, the amount of *time* spent, as well as our intake and application of these details has proceeded along very different paths. The King uses us in the outside world to live among the people whether they know the King or not. Sometimes we are sent only to casually visit, sometimes to speak the words on our heart, sometimes to confront, sometimes just to come alongside. But in any and every event or circumstance, long or short, we can depend on Him to use what we're thinking, deciding, and doing—all to accomplish *His* purposes and His goals. *Our* goal is to tell people about the King and what He has done but especially to encourage them to ask for a changed heart granted by the King's Spirit. Then they should rely upon the King's Son to save them. He brings each new adopted child to have a life inside the Kingdom, to dwell there with the King forever, rather than remain in darkness on the outside forever separated from the King.

We can only plant the seeds. We must depend upon the King to provide sunshine and water and, indeed, to germinate each seed, bringing it to life and developing all new growth, just as He did for you and me. While traveling outside the Kingdom, there will be groups we join as we praise the King, and amidst these groups, there will be some who do not truly know or understand. To navigate these moments of sharing, you will be able to take your own Guidebook along to keep studying the words that construct each room of every palace in the Kingdom—a total of 1,188 rooms! You may think you can never know everything, or be completely prepared, and you are correct. Yet, the necessary details of what to say and do will become evident. As you forget about yourself and ask for the King's help—through His Spirit—you will become more and more able.

As you consult your Guidebook, you will find it easier to locate necessary information for further review, and you will be filled with a desire to study and learn more of the King's ways, developing your understanding by building precept upon precept. You will also have access to the special communication center that works within your mind, allowing you to communicate with the King at all times and giving you the capacity to memorize or otherwise remember important precepts. Sometimes, you will receive answers you recognize immediately, while at other times the King will allow you to figure things out for yourself, or even not be given answers at all. Remember how in so many different rooms we learned about our ancestors asking *why* the King was not hearing, *why* He was not answering, or *why* was He delaying? Now you understand, and you will also be prepared to *persevere*. Carol starts singing "In His Time," and I join her, impressed at how appropriate the song is for this moment.

Dr. Gene Baillie

The King has given you this independence, purpose, teaching, and all these goals—not only for His glory but for *your own good and growth*. You will have direct access to His Kingdom, allowing you to go out and return as the Spirit leads. I would not be surprised if, even today, the King assigns you to become involved in the work His children do outside His Kingdom. I have been assigned to the outside kingdoms many times. Each time has been quite different. Sometimes a person accompanies me back to the gate and is disappointed not to be allowed in. I realize they have learned the words to say but have not had the necessary heart change. The King has me return here for encouragement and as an encourager, sometimes by being a docent to guide people through the rooms of a particular palace. I would love to tell you about times outside and times in other palaces throughout this Kingdom, but they are stories for another day.

Now it is *time* to enter room 91. I feel like I'm turning over a new "leaf." Prior to this point I was learning mostly for myself, confirming my adoption and my secure dwelling within the safety of this Kingdom. Now, however, I not only see the need but also have a rejuvenated desire to travel beyond the Kingdom to proclaim what I have learned. The previous room showed me the short length of life I have. All the revelation, teaching, and learning I have received has a greater purpose far beyond my own well-being. Indeed, one of my purposes in the outside world is to boldly encourage others to seek this place. The visual streams of words in this room confirm my thoughts: *whoever* dwells in the shelter of the Most High will receive all the benefits this Kingdom of light and life has to offer.

When I go out, I will speak to people about how this place provides refuge and security—they will be protected by the shadow of the almighty King, who will be like a shield about them. As in room 3, He is like a shield protecting His people from all harm and dread. I become attuned to more of the words creating this room, and I see there are angels all around, protecting those who are part of this

Kingdom. The King loves me, and He will rescue those who are His chosen even though they still live in the outside world. I will be an instrument He uses to draw them in. He will give both myself and His newfound children a length of days to satisfy Him. I desire to use every second of the time He has granted me, so I may tell others about His salvation. Just as I experienced salvation, He will save others. Because my King loves me and has given me the ability to love, I am able to love Him and also others. I believe this is an important part of what the King means by saying He is indwelling me. His blessing is not for me alone, *but that I might be a blessing.*

We proceed to room 92, and I realize more fully how each of us needs to etch the truth and principles we have learned into our minds, remember them, and even memorize portions of the words creating, decorating, and describing this and other rooms. Then, when we are on the outside, we will be able to recall them for situations we encounter. First, as I awake each morning, then all through the day and again at night, I must remember to give thanks to the King as I recall what He has done for me and all He has given me. It makes me glad to thank my King in *all* circumstances. Second, I desire do the work He has given me because I see the works of His hands, and I comprehend some of His deep thoughts toward me. Wherever I am, I will make music—as I blow on an instrument or my own humming, as I sing to the King or tell others of what I have experienced. As we explore this room, a holographic film suddenly becomes visible before our eyes, showing weeds sprouting up, blossoming, then being destroyed. This is in contrast with the next holographic clip, showing a palm tree that keeps sprouting new branches. Instead of dying, we watch as it is uprooted then transplanted into the King's garden, where it continues to sprout, being fruitful in every season into its old age. It is a beautiful reminder of how I was transplanted and moved to my permanent home, bearing fruit in every season.

Dr. Gene Baillie

    I have just become comfortable with visiting rooms mostly in their number order, but now I see a sign pointing to a doorway saying, "Visit these rooms as you exit." We enter the passageway giving access to rooms 136–139. We decide to visit each of these rooms in turn. Wow! Room 136 has an extremely compelling light-and-sound show. A banner pops up, and multiple colors flash around its borders. We read and join in singing each phrase of a few words followed by, "His steadfast love endures forever; His banner over us is love." This banner assuring us of the King's steadfast love is repeated on each of many other banners appearing in turn, with the choir first echoing the wording on each banner: "Give thanks to the King"; "He alone does great wonders"; "He created the heavens, earth, and waters"; "He who made the sun, moon, and stars"; and at least 20 more!

    Entering room 137 reveals a sad group of people in a prison camp beside a river. Their captors ask them to sing one of their songs from their home country, but their fingers are unable to produce music from their instruments. They are just too sad, and their tongues seem to be stuck to the roofs of their mouths. Some relevant history gives us more perspective. At one time in the past, the King's people became rebellious, honoring the kings beyond their borders then becoming enslaved to these kings. These circumstances soon led to some of the King's citizens rebelling against one of the foreign kings, so the foreign king broke down a section of their kingdom wall and destroyed our King's temple. Many were taken captive to the far-off land, which we hear in this room is called "Babylon."

    We suddenly become aware of how many dusty, unused musical instruments are lying around. The people who have been taken captive are clearly sad, and even though their captors encourage them to make music, they continually resist picking up an instrument, knowing their fingers lack motivation—they have no desire to play.

The King's 19th Palace

Those who try to sing simply cannot raise a true note. I recall a few verses of writing I read in the Ezra Palace about a portion of these captives being released to return to their kingdom to rebuild the temple—but only after 70 years of captivity! Then, as we move to room 138, the view that meets our eyes reveals the King's people as they rise up in response to answered prayer. With their strength increased, they find the will to sing, giving thanks for the steadfast love of the King. They seem revitalized, having gained the understanding He will fulfill His purpose for each one of them.

Although I could spend many days visiting room 139, a shorter summary will have to suffice for now. Carol and I see words literally upholding this room, quickly realizing the King has searched each of us and knows us completely, including each thought. He holds us up and also protects us from every side. We can never escape the King's presence, no matter where we go or what our current situation might be. The whole earth is full of His wonders, including the manner in which He formed each of us at conception, and with specific intentions for the span of life He gives. He has numbered each day of life on earth. He is the Wonder of all wonders, and to name these wonders would be more than all the grains of sand everywhere throughout the whole world (I have heard there are about 400,000 grains in a single handful!). As we recognize the imperfections within ourselves, and throughout everyone and everything around us, we start dreaming about and desiring *His* perfection. We can seek refuge, but no one will find it without the guiding hand of the King and His Son.

Carol and I discuss how these side rooms all have presented a path of connected truth and deliver a vital message. We agree it is the heritage we pass on that is vitally important to remember as we proclaim His message of truth. I also recall the many connections to the rooms of other palaces within the Kingdom, and I make a note to tour them in more detail at a later time.

I must tell you two things you might not have noted and I just realized. First, we have not needed the virtual-reality glasses in many recent rooms. Everything has become progressively accessible within our very being somehow, so we have not missed any detail to perceive and drink in! It is something like going on a trip, then certain memories of events just come "alive." Second, I can but tell you of my feelings of a spiritual world that is so real. For instance, I know and sense that both the "inside" and "outside" kingdoms are not always with defined borders. Many times opportunities in the outside kingdom are in the very space around me. Again, it is something like the saying, "You don't have to go to the mission field at all; the mission field comes often to you."

All I know is that it is different but similar to how I perceive when I communicate in prayer with my King. I feel the King's presence; and it seems as if He is not only suggesting I go out into the surrounding kingdoms, but His strong right hand will direct me to those in need of Him, sometimes with only a moment of notice. Even though I do not feel ready, and although evil will surely battle against me forcefully, I know I can depend on the King's armament, comprising of His Word, His angels, and His army—of which I am a soldier. He will lead the battle, and He will lead me in the way everlasting.

We keep following the exit signs, and I fully expect Carol and I will exit outside the Kingdom to be tested. Instead, we find we are entering room 93 to continue our journey of training and readiness.

This is a small room, but the words it reflects speak of the King's great power. The King established the world and all the people dwelling therein. All of His creation is giving Him honor, and we are to do the same, for His decrees are trustworthy. His Word is to be trusted completely for the length of days He gives to each of us.

Carol opens a door set against the far wall of the room, and when I join her, we find we are in room 94. A holographic film of various outside kingdoms is projected before us. The clip is suddenly lit by an extreme brightness that we immediately recognize—it is the King shining out brighter than the sun as He judges all the wicked of the surrounding kingdoms. In their ignorance, they think He does not see them. I must tell them to be more discerning. It is the King who made their ears—He is the one who can hear and who *gives them the ability* to hear. It is the King who formed their eyes, and He is the one who can see. It is He who enables them to see and provides them with His light for this purpose. And there is at least one more dimension—I need to tell them He is also the One who knows their every thought. He is preparing me to inform and instruct them.

Among these lost souls will be some evil people who will be given the ability to listen and see and who will turn their attention and intentions to the King. Although the King knows, I do not know who they are. My duty is to not be silent, but instead to speak out, confronting, sometimes boldly and other times gently. It is sometimes a scary and discomforting feeling, but I can depend upon the King to not only hold me up and comfort me, but also to *change some of them* just as He changed me. He will open their eyes to see and their ears to hear truth. They surmise they can do whatever they think is right in their own eyes. Wrong! They think they can follow only their own dreams and desires. Also wrong! Those who will not recognize the authority of the King are sadly misguided. I turn to my wife and see her also grappling with conflicting emotions. She is overjoyed at those who accept the King's love but also greatly saddened by those who reject Him. We exit the room, discussing how we can share with more people how we were drawn into the safe, loving arms of our King.

Chapter 15

The King satisfies us with good, and all He does is good. His good is working in us perfection, completion, and usefulness for His purposes (based on Psalm 103:1–5).

"I sometimes think about how different my spiritual life was before we found these many different ways to access the King's palaces." It is twilight, and I had just come out onto the porch to sit with Carol. I ponder a bit, thinking about what she said. *There was a time when, in my ignorance, I simply accepted an uneventful spiritual life—if ever there was one at all. But since the King rescued me from that darkness and drudgery, I have increasingly felt great joy, recognizing my certain purpose on this earth.*

"I sometimes think about how much we have learned since my initial introduction to this new way of accessing just one of the King's palaces in the Appalachian foothills. I consider how blessed we are to have gained such valuable insights into His Kingdom. Going through a doorway on an audio-visual journey really does reveal the truth of the message contained within each specific room—it is like being there, and better than even our trip to Israel, Jordan, and Egypt." We both sit a while, and I meditate on our many journeys, thinking about the rooms we have seen and the wisdom contained within every one. I turn my head to catch Carol's attention, but she is already looking at me.

The King's 19th Palace

"We were born for such a time as this," Carol says softly, smiling. "Our dinner will be ready in a few minutes." I stand and reach for her hand, we turn together, and as we enter our front door, we find ourselves in room 95.

Although I am still safely within the confines of the Kingdom, exploring the many dazzling rooms of this 19th Palace, a surge of excitement wells up within me—this continuing preparation so I might respond appropriately, speaking the King's message and acting out His will on earth. I suddenly see an image of myself projected onto a nearby wall, and I watch, fascinated. I'm walking about, talking to people who will listen, telling them about the King who created everything and who chooses to save many. I encourage people to discuss the King's plans for their life on earth, and also to study His Word so they know their own part in His master plan. I start inviting people to join me as we enter into specifically designed places where we worship and bow down, and then kneel before the King our Maker. We listen to the words from His Guidebook being proclaimed, and I am grateful for those who have heard the message and acted upon it. All will hear, but only those whose ears are unstopped by the King will be able to truly hear, respond, and comprehend.

The image fades to white, and I recover from the joy this scenario has induced. I am about to launch into an explanation of what I saw, but Carol stops me—she saw herself in a similar scene declaring the King's message of salvation. We talk about how grateful we are to have had our hearts of stone turned to flesh, that we, too, might enter into the King's rest. We enter room 96, and I seem to float as I walk—I am still in a place of worship, blessed by the knowledge of being useful to my King. We join our voices in song to bless the King's name, singing "The Splendor of the King!"

We hear our own voices speak of how great He is in all His splendor, His majesty, strength, and beauty. These characteristics seem to emanate from the very structure of this room and are also coming forth from us. Yet another video is projected onto the wall in front of us, but this time Carol and I are both present in the high-definition hologram. Among a group of people, we bring our gifts before the King. As I watch, I realize the gift I unwrap and am offering Him is my entire being—I offer him my very self in its entirety. It thrills me to watch myself dedicating all I am to Him. It goes way beyond the external time, talent, and treasure factors shaping my life—I am turning over all my abilities and desires. Watching ourselves and many others bow before the King to offer our gifts enables me to become fully cognizant of the fact *He* is the One who provides us with every good thing. We are simply offering back to Him everything within us He uses to increase His—and our—family.

The clip continues, and we speak more of this good news about the King, how He saves, and all of the wonders He has performed. The projected image suddenly increases in size, filling the entire wall—as if to make the King's splendor entirely plain to me, projecting His goodness to the very depth of my heart. I see a background of thunder and lightning then trees swaying back and forth with fireworks going off in the heavens. Every part of the King's creation is praising Him. We watch in amazement until the screen fades, then stand for a moment, breathing in the beauty of what we have witnessed—all of creation praising our King. Finding ourselves entering room 97, I see the outside world being projected onto all four walls in surrounding and ever-changing kaleidoscopic effect.

In some scenarios I am seemingly observing these worldly images, but in others I seem to also be among the people portrayed. A myriad of objects and people are streaming in from all the edges to the center. Within the center clouds and darkness surround an overwhelming source of light. Flashes like lightning reveal people in the periphery, standing in terror or in awe. Some are cast away, while others seem to be struck by a bright ray of light, then suddenly

The King's 19th Palace

brought into the middle, where they begin marching along with a gathering crowd. I can literally see their new hearts beating as they rejoice. They are marching toward the Kingdom gates, following the Light, and we are in the midst of this throng, singing praises to our glorious King.

We realize we are now marching into room 98. Our crowd is singing, and people are loudly proclaiming the wonderful things the King has done, how He saved each of them, and how He continues to show His steadfast love and reveal His truth. Trumpets and horns now join the shouting and rejoicing. Yet again, the edges and background of the scene we are in reveals trees, and now even rivers, swaying back and forth on all sides, seeming to clap their hands. The hills and the distant ocean roar! Everything is praising the King of kings. Again I have a sense we are moving into another room, and sure enough, we are entering a really large room. I look at the room number on the door and see that rooms 99 and 100 are one big room.

We are still among the growing throng of marchers. As I look first to my right, I see a vision of our King sitting on a throne, holy and high above the people. He is reigning with fairness, judgment, and righteousness. Then I turn to the left and see our throng of people raising loud voices of joyous praise to the King, proclaiming to all the world, "Yahweh is King—He made us! We are His people and we have come within these, His gates, with thanksgiving and praise. We give all thanks to Him for He is good, and His steadfast love pervades all generations." I see we are on the move again, entering another large space that reflects rooms 101 and 102.

As we progress within the throng of people in this continuing, virtual vision, I see the throne room opens onto a multitude of encircling rooms. So whichever room we walk into, somehow we are still facing the front of the throne, feeling the presence of the King. Carol and I lift our voices along with the vibrant host of worshippers singing to the King about His steadfast love, His judgments, His mighty acts, His truths, and His unwavering integrity. The song we sing then changes to "Blessed Assurance, the King's Son Is Mine!" I turn my gaze in the opposite direction, behind the gathered throng of worshippers, and what I see saddens me. In the distance, beyond the Kingdom border I witness the ongoing plight of people fleeing into the surrounding darkness, as though they are being thrown away. I hear their cries of agony and hopelessness, but my focus shifts as I also see many people being plucked from the darkness and brought into the light. I rejoice as I see they are energized by the Light, able to withstand the evil forces of the dark. I watch, captivated, as their clothes literally fall off, then each person's garments are replaced with a white robe, after which they start joining our throng. In joy, all I can say is, "Wow!"

We proceed toward the next open doorway, and as we enter room 103, I am reminded when I, too, was plucked from the muddy and miry pit, having my dirty clothes removed and flung away. In retrospect I realize it was me who dug that pit—I added mud to it, and *I* am the one who fell into it. I *loved* the mud; making mud pies was my delight! In all truth, I *deserved* to be cast into the outer darkness, but the compassionate King chose to lift me up and adopt me. I watch as the old clothes of those being brought into the light are now flung into the sea to a depth of fathoms beyond my wildest perception. I see a spinning earth whose motion is continually carrying old garments to the east, and I realize they will *never* reach the west! All this reminds me again of the King's steadfast love. He changed me, and I desire to obey Him in all ways, bringing Him a blessing as I do His will and His work.

Carol takes my hand as we enter room 104. I look back toward the central throne room, encircled by these many rooms, and I sense the King clothed in white light. My adoration for Him knows no limit, but even as I stand before Him in His marvelous presence, a sudden eruption of light and sound interrupts my moment of reverence. I hear laughter, filled with pure, delighted joy—we are

The King's 19th Palace

witnessing a show beyond imagination. The mountains and all of creation surrounding this amphitheater of rooms is lighting up with the supernatural radiance of our King. Colored geysers of water start erupting into the atmosphere to celebrate His presence, while a variety of animals add their voices in worship to the King and the surrounding trees are filled with singing birds. We quickly realize we are in the thick of a joyous festival, so we join with the vast throng who are feasting on a range of culinary delights. As each table is emptied, an image of what appears to be the King's hand fills it once more, providing a fresh range of delectable nourishment.

Between bites I turn with joy to welcome those joining us, but from the corner of my eye, I witness something that makes me sad—as yet again I see terrified people disappearing into the darkness beyond the amphitheater. What a mixture of emotions I am continually experiencing and enduring, knowing all things work together and have His purpose for those who love, believe, and trust in our King. Replete with good food and filled with wonder, we leave the room, hungry to experience more of His goodness. We proceed toward the next open doorway, where the people we march with are removing their virtual-reality glasses, realizing again, we have not needed any.

We enter room 105, and I find a sturdy couch, sinking into it as I assess my current situation. I hear the celestial choir singing the opening verse of the room: "Oh give thanks to the Lord; call upon his name; make known his deeds among the peoples!" I am immediately inspired by this directive to share His truth. Though I find myself in a room of the King's palace, I feel the urge to be outside, talking about and sharing how the King not only created us, but how He also *can* and *does* change us. I know I am repeating these principles many times, but I need the repetition—just as we see in these rooms—to make known all His deeds and wondrous works. None of my work was able to bring me to this place, but now that I am His adopted child, He is doing His work through me—and I feel *compelled* to do His work. I need to tell people on the outside to rejoice in seeking the King and His strength. They cannot save themselves and need to quit their wandering. The King can release them from the tyranny of their current leader and every evil situation. I need to explain all the King did for our forefathers, His covenant promises, what He did and is doing for me, and how He brought and continues to bring His children out of darkness and captivity with joy and singing.

Because I have seen all these ever-changing rooms and have noticed their many different ways of communicating to me, I have also become aware of the continuing changes occurring within me. I recognize "I once was lost but now have been found," and drastically changed for the better by my King. I have many songs swirling in my head, reminding me of where I was and what He did: "I Know in Whom I Believe"; "I Am Convinced and Am Able to Guard What He Has Entrusted to Me"; "I Am Leaning on the Everlasting Arms." I am growing in knowledge and understanding, not only for my benefit and blessing, but again in preparation for me to also be a blessing. As I learn more about the King, His creation, and the outside kingdoms, I recognize how any evil thoughts, words, and deeds—which are continually being removed from me—are all adding to my greater understanding of how I am to actively engage and willingly participate in doing anything and everything the King requires of me here and in the outside kingdoms.

The training and seminar rooms in all the King's palaces have enabled me to see myself actively participating in a multitude of situations. Every room has prepared and is increasingly preparing me to say the right things and to act appropriately when speaking to others about what the King is doing, while simultaneously reflecting His truths in my own life. These rooms also give me the ability to rightly discern my future life with my King, enriching this life with certain hope. I am gaining a greater understanding of what my faith in the King consists of. I have learned the King's name is *Yahweh*—meaning, in part, the "Ever-Present, Always-Acting-and-Solving King." You can ask or wonder anything, and He is *always* the "I AM" solution. For instance, if I am dealing with fear, it is He who says, "I AM your comfort and peace." His Son is named *Jeshua*, meaning "the King saves."

Remember, although there have been no written tests, you have been and will continually be tested, to be approved—like a workman able to accomplish each building task and a runner able to finish the race, ultimately reaching the prize of your upward calling.

Room 106, simply put, is another history room filled with many objects and testimonies pertaining to the King's people. They seem to demonstrate obedience for a season, but this is soon followed by rebellion and disobedience, which appears to be a recurring theme throughout their history. We see their failure to follow His directions, and their failure to acknowledge His power. Time and again they cried out to the King in their distress, requesting His mercy, and He granted what they asked. They also tried to change their circumstances by relying on their own work and power, as they thought best, but were thwarted in their arrogance. We would do well to learn these lessons presented and to acknowledge that when we say, "The King's will be done!" it truly is the King who is in charge . . . not us. He is good, and His steadfast love endures forever.

*Lamentations 3:21–24: "But this I call to mind, and therefore I have hope: The steadfast love of the L*ORD *never ceases; His mercies never come to an end; they are new every morning; great is His faithfulness. My soul says, 'The L*ORD *is my portion; therefore I will hope in Him.'" (Author's translation)*

Chapter 16

The chosen, redeemed, and ransomed of the King have everlasting joy as they sing His praises (based on Isaiah 35:10). All things the King provides and all He does are for our good and His glory. We can count on Him for His steadfast love and faithfulness. We will bless Him forevermore (based on Psalm 115:1, 18).

"Gene!"

I turn swiftly, hearing a slightly urgent edge to Carol's tone. A woman in the aisle beside me also turns quickly, so Carol switches to a whisper, beckoning me with a forefinger. "Come see what I found." The woman and I exchange a smile as I walk to the end of the aisle, where Carol awaits my arrival with a sense of excitement.

We've stopped off in a convenience store in Galesburg, Illinois, to pick up a quick and easy dinner. We're returning to South Carolina from our visit to Nebraska, stopped here to see ancestor gravestones, and will be overnighting at a Bed and Breakfast. She points to a glowing Hebrew symbol on what appears to be a door in a back corner of the store. It pulsates, alternating between bright and dim. I emit a low whistle of surprise, then we high-five for her astute observation.

"I was reflecting on our recent experience in your old root cellar, which turned my thoughts to our room visits. I happened to be

The King's 19th Palace

staring at this door, and when the symbol appeared, I realized we're being given another opportunity to explore."

As I have been used to doing previously, I excitedly place my palm over the glowing inscription, and we suddenly find ourselves in an arched tunnel with a large wooden door standing open before us. A bronze plaque on the room door has the number 107 inscribed on it. Carol leads the way.

In many of the previous rooms we have visited in the 19th Palace, we have either heard, read, or seen the King's steadfast love manifested in numerous ways. This room, however, seems to distill and concentrate all these experiences into an almost tangible essence. Carol and I both feel the King's presence as He teaches us truth about this steadfast love. As we focus on specific sentences streaming toward us, taking in with all our senses the timeless meaning they convey, we realize His unwavering love has so many manifestations and aspects. It is felt but not describable, is limitless but we cannot fully comprehend it. His love does indeed endure *through all, and in all, forever.* We watch and see how His love plucks and delivers people from the darkness and from their wandering ways, putting them on a straight road to the gates of this Kingdom. We stand transfixed, as holographic scenes begin to appear before us, and in the first we see the King removing a sin-filled heart and replacing it with a new heart.

The scene switches, and we see a prisoner huddled in the corner of a dark cell, but then the King appears, and we see the purest stream of love radiating out from Him. The bright, golden stream of love shatters the chains keeping the prisoner bound in the corner, and as he rises to his feet, the shackles fall from his wrists and ankles. The bright stream of love fills the once-dark prison, dispelling and removing all evidence of the prisoner's previous record. We witness snippets of his past life—the path of devious and deadly disobedience he once walked starts to fly by us then quickly dissolves when encompassed by the King's steadfast love. I take Carol's hand as scenes different for each of our own lives start unfolding, and I realize it is *His* love that also changed us, healed us, and redeemed us from our quite different but sinful ways—ways that deprived us of so many good things. He removed us from a sinful path of certain death, with its dreadful and subsequent eternal separation from our King. He helped us to repent, to make a 180-degree turn to follow Him and stay on His path.

Another image appears, and this time we perceive His steadfast love rescuing us from a ship certain to sink in a stormy sea. We watch the frantic but impossible effort of the crew as they try to control the ship. Then we see the winds calm and the sea become smooth, and drifting into this calm, we hear voices singing, "Love lifted me!" Yet again, I feel the overwhelming presence of my King's committed and steadfast love for me. The holographic scenes disappear, and in their place, we see a large group of people gathering—we're both cognizant they symbolize all the King's redeemed and adopted children, and we join the throng gladly, wholeheartedly agreeing with them that the steadfast love of our King knows no bounds.

Before us is a connecting doorway to room 108, and when we enter, we hear music and singing but it seems to be reaching us from the four different directions. All the songs are about the King's steadfast love, and there is one coming from the room we have just left, as well as another connected room—room 57. We turn our attention back to room 108, but the words we see and hear in this room we have encountered before from another adjacent room, also connected to these three—room 60. Yet another room is connected to these four—room 89—and emanating from all these rooms are so many reminders of love and songs about love, confirming the indelible truth of our King's steadfast love!

Feeling energized by these convergent messages of the King's love, we suddenly find ourselves in room 109 . . . but I must warn you—although this room is for the good of all the King's children, it is rather shocking. In the previous several rooms, we heard about the King's steadfast love but not from this angle! The words we see streaming toward us allow us to see ourselves on the outside of this Kingdom we call home. We see ourselves asking the King to deliver us from times when we struggle to see Him, and from a place where we do not think He is for us, guiding us, or helping us in any way. In these difficult times, we may ask the question: "Where is our 'big D' Defender," as all we are able to encounter—and try to conquer—are our "little d's."

When we travel to the outside kingdoms, we will experience the "d's" of disappointment and distress, and there will be times when we feel deprived, discarded, and dishonored. Having experienced these feelings firsthand, and feeling totally alone, my advice to you is to simply allow all these negative thoughts and situations to be a reminder of your crucial need to be prepared. Your own constantly changing transformation is vital! Especially as you go out to confront the suffocating domination of sin and its effects on your choices and the actions that follow them, as well as the choices made by other people and their concomitant actions.

We move into room 110, and in this room we realize an earthly king foresaw the appointed time wherein the King's Son would take His seat at the King's right hand. We marvel at the power contained within this room—our King is still King on His throne, and He will judge every nation outside of His Kingdom. He is unchangeable and will forever be our priest, interceding on our behalf.

Room 111 has a festive atmosphere of praise established by the celestial song that greets us. We are to give thanks to our King and know that He is forever righteous, gracious, and compassionate. He is trustworthy and will carry out His covenant, which He established with His chosen children. As I am reminded of these things, I realize I have not only learned many essential truths—due to my increasing knowledge base—but I also have more understanding.

Some of my understanding now approaches the much-prized goal of wisdom, yet this is founded on knowing that the King alone has true wisdom.

When we enter room 112, we hear an often-repeated verse that echoes throughout the chambers of the 19th Palace, repeated in different ways and in many of His other palaces too: "Blessed is the man who fears the Lord, who greatly delights in his commandments!" Embracing the opportunity to sing His praises, we once again admit our reverential fear of the King, and our great delight in His commandments. We both recognize our many blessings are ultimately established on having an awesome but righteous fear for our King. We also delight in doing His commandments. What a joyful honor to be one of His chosen and adopted children. I feel immensely blessed as I recall the recent events of His light shining into the darkness, plucking so many souls from those dreadful shadows to become His children. I am thankful yet again for an overwhelming desire to travel beyond the Kingdom gates to speak the details of His truth, goodness, righteousness, judgment, and of His steadfast love. Thanksgiving is to be every day, as we are thankful in all circumstances.

When we exit the room, we are back in the arched tunnel where our palace journey began here in Illinois. To our right is the large wooden door we first entered, but wait ... to our left is another door. The bronze plaque on the door reads "113 to 116." Carol opens the door, and we enter a large, open room giving us access to these connected rooms, which all open centrally from the four corners under one roof. As we cross the invisible borders between the rooms, the song of the celestial choir shifts accordingly, and we hear the words of each separate room being sung in each corner of the large room. After moving between the rooms, we soon realize they are rooms of review and encouragement. We stop often to sit and praise the King's name, joining with the choir to sing His praises in the various ways presented in each room.

The King's 19th Palace

We feel His presence surrounding us, and as the weight of His glory fills the room, we sit on a couch in the center of the room, which rotates slowly so we see each room again with every circuit. A number of images start appearing before our eyes. We see mountains skipping like rams and seas swirling around them, rising up before the voice of the King to become dry land. We see and hear massive rocks colliding, causing huge sparks to flare up like lightning, which then turn immediately into geysers of water erupting into the sky. We watch, fascinated, as these colossal wonders are followed by seeing people being raised from the dust, who come to sit right beside us. But then we see images of silver and gold being made by other outside people, who have shaped these metals into human and animal likenesses. The images have mouths that cannot speak, eyes that cannot see, ears that cannot hear, noses that cannot smell, hands that cannot feel, and feet that cannot walk.

They seem so real that I become curious. I feel I am being drawn to the presence of these idols and the people worshipping them. Yet, the King has given me the proper words to speak and the correct thoughts to think, so I can easily say to the people worshipping these idols, "This is all a lie!" Just as I learned in the very first room of this palace, I am well prepared to "Keep on walking." Carol catches my eye, and together we rise and walk away from the shiny metal images. The King keeps our feet from stumbling. We are both aroused from this dreamy vision of appearing images, feeling exhausted but also so thankful for what we have experienced in these four rooms. We stand together, still praising, and then we begin to sing, "Not to us, O King, but to your name belongs glory because of Your steadfast love, Your truth, Your awesome power, Your salvation."

We are back into the long, arched tunnel, and once again to our left, we find another door with two room numbers printed on the wooden frame: 117–118. When we enter, we realize room 117 is the smaller room, and it opens up into the larger room, 118. I remain in the smaller room where I join in singing praise to my King.

While in this smaller room, an interesting vision or dream appears in my mind as I hear the words sung. I see myself joining numerous other people who are ready to proclaim the King's steadfast love and truth. The King is my all in all! He is my help—what can anyone possibly do to me? As if to answer my question, I suddenly become aware of a group of people coming in from room 118, surrounding me, and who clearly have evil intentions. But in confirmation of His protection and loving care for me, the King prevents them from advancing. They are like bees coming at me, but they are quickly driven off by an intense, crackling fire. I realize I, too, have been given strength from the King to fend them off. I start singing, "He is my strength and my song, He is my salvation." He has taught me so lovingly and so thoroughly. I feel ready and prepared to march outside, so I can speak to people about the King, about His truth, and His Kingdom. I am also grateful for the privilege of being able to march back into His Kingdom with all the other righteous when our day's work is done.

I then move into the larger room but wait! This room 118 has a familiar look—it is unlike most of the rooms we have visited in this 19th Palace—it resembles a cave that has become a construction site, and the floor has been cut down to the bedrock foundation. It also has a soft light permeating the atmosphere. I see now a large stone has been brought in and is being placed as the headstone or cornerstone of the King's house. "Wow! This is where my palace adventure truly began!" My voice echoes through the chamber, and my wife's bright, bubbly laughter of recognition rebounds off the walls.

I approach the massive cornerstone rising from the surface of the bedrock, and just like the thoughts which rose in my mind when I first visited the cave of light, I marvel at the smooth-grained texture of the granite. I recall the rising panic I felt when I was unable to find the opening through which I had entered, yet how the soft light permeating the atmosphere had such a soothing effect on me, dispersing all feelings of panic. Now again, as I feel the soft light bathing me, it fills me with peace, while at the same time I hear the celestial choir singing these words: "Blessed is he who comes in the name of the Lord! We bless you from the house of the Lord. The Lord is God, and He has made His Light to shine upon us." I am filled with wonder at everything I have learned while exploring this awesome palace my King constructed. I continue each day to understand more and more why the Lord has blessed me as He led my journey to this very room, now again by a different "entrance." I know it has been an important journey in my spiritual growth, and that the time is fast approaching when Carol and I, along with the chosen of our families and all the King's children, will be marching to Zion—the name of the King's dwelling on the hill of this Kingdom. Today and every day, I love singing, "This is the day the Lord has made, we will rejoice and be glad in it."

As we exit this room, I take one long, lingering look at the Cornerstone bathed in the soft light, and I send my heartfelt thanks to the King for enabling me to become a living stone. I am so utterly grateful to have become an integral part of the spiritual house God is building—one of the crucial blocks of living stone populating His Kingdom!

We enter room 119 further along the arched tunnel, and as we walk, it becomes evident this is the largest room by far in the palace. It is actually a series of 22 alcoves (really each a small room in its own right), with each of these recesses displaying eight study or review points to walk in His ways. Each point teaches us of the results when we keep, follow, and adhere to the King's written instructions or rules, using a series of twelve repeated synonyms: His precepts, His teachings, His law, His Word, His way, and His righteousness, as well as His statutes, commandments, judgments, testimonies, and His faithfulness or truth. For several moments, my mind reverts to previous days when I looked for the way, the truth, and the life in my own way and used my own strength. I sought specific treasures, including money, love, possessions, health, and the ability to travel freely—all to provide what I thought would be a full life. I was acquiring and delighting in all things, going far beyond need, and I held everything tightly, trying to maintain control.

I loved my family and friends, but I loved myself—and my ability to control and accumulate possessions—much more. I did not know the King or His Word. But now I count on the King to teach me, so I can remember His way—truly the proper path to walk. I begin to sing "Nearer My King to Thee." As I contemplate what I have been taught, I also remember times of learning I found quite comfortable within this Kingdom, working in the King's gardens, and helping with the preparation and delivery of meals—being and living His Word—to those in need. *And* I remember the exact day the King assigned me to go till His "garden" outside the gate, to meet and mix with those outside, who—like the previous me—did not have a clue about the joys of this Kingdom.

Now my attention snaps back to this room, aware the writing in this room is strongly stamping into my mind the tremendous usefulness of His Word in all aspects of my life. I encourage you to dwell on these many alcoves as I will mention a few I especially like: As I learn more and more of His teachings, I gain greater understanding of how His Word blesses me when I walk according to His teaching. I recognize how keeping His Word can make a young man's path pure and how we need to hide His Word in our hearts in order not to sin against the King. His Word is a lamp for my feet and a light for my path—my whole heart desires to follow His Word, knowing He will keep me from wandering. He opens my eyes to see all the wondrous things in His Word, revealing how the Word gives me understanding, so I may follow and keep His Word. He turns my eyes from looking at worthless things, instilling within me knowledge that the whole world is full of His steadfast love!

I recognize how He alone has given me the desire to meditate on His Word all day long. His Word is sweet in my mouth like honey, and I desire to understand it, as it keeps me from wrong ways. I have great peace, especially because His Word keeps me from stumbling. In the last alcove, I am compared to a wandering, lost sheep, which inspires me to sing, "Prone to wander, King, seek and save me." In all these alcoves, I see the sum of His Word is truth.

Chapter 17

The King is my keeper. He keeps me from all evil, He has kept me all my life, and He will keep my going out and coming in forevermore (based on Psalm 121:5–8).

I build in vain unless the King directs the building of my spiritual house (based on Psalm 127:1).

Great is the King and greatly to be praised. He is full of grace and mercy; He is loving and good (based on Psalm 145:3, 8–9).

A decision is made to visit again the cave in the Appalachian foothills where this exciting, inspiring, and revealing journey into the King's 19th Palace ultimately began. We present our plan to Eric and Mary, asking if they will be able to join us. We propose a time during school vacation, hoping Elizabeth and John will also join us to explore the remaining rooms in the palace. Our request is given on short notice, with only two weeks before the school vacation starts, but Eric and Mary are thrilled at the prospect, green-lighting our expedition immediately.

Two weeks pass quickly while we prepare for our journey, and when the big day finally arrives, we leave home in convoy. I look at my rearview mirror and see Eric at the wheel of his pickup, Mary in the passenger seat, and Elizabeth and John chatting animatedly in the rear seats of Eric's double-cab. I give Eric a thumbs-up, and he lifts his thumb in response. I ease out of the driveway onto the road and start singing a song of praise, releasing the pent-up excitement that has been building over the past few days. We sing a range of songs celebrating the joy and wonder of being a part of the King's family, and we arrive at our destination late morning.

Eric pulls his pickup close to mine, and we unpack our gear for our stay. I pick the overgrown, narrow path less traveled, staying close to the river, walking single file until we reach the overhang where I originally found the flint-tipped arrows and the reed blowgun. We eat sandwiches in the shade along the riverbank and cool off in the river before climbing up to the overhang. Everyone collects firewood as we climb, and when we arrive, we squeeze through the opening into the cave behind the overhang. We deposit our firewood in a heap next to the ash from my previous campfires, then set up our campsite. John and Elizabeth are champing at the bit, so without further ado, we set off along the underground river course.

We reach the crystal cave, and the newcomers are absolutely enthralled by the majestic beauty of this glittering cavern. Elizabeth spots the amethyst first—she had heard Carol speak enthusiastically about how a simple twist of the protruding crystal opens a doorway into the chamber of light.

"Papa, can I please turn the stone to open the door?"

Eric and Mary are still exploring the chamber, so I answer diplomatically, "You certainly may, Elizabeth. Let's just wait for your mom and dad to join us—it's always a good idea to stick close together when underground, as you well know." Elizabeth looks slightly crestfallen at having to wait, but she recovers quickly, pleased to know she will have the honor of granting us all access to the King's palace. Mary joins the rest of us as I note John looks like I felt on my first excursion into this cavern—like a poor man in a goldmine! Elizabeth looks at me beseechingly now, so I give her my nod of approval, and she steps up to the amethyst. She turns it to the right then squeals delightedly when the door starts sliding, grating loudly as it opens. We all stand in awe, bathed in the soft, gentle ambiance emanating from the chamber of light.

I step forward and take Elizabeth's hand, and the others follow my example until we all stand before the opening, linked by our hands. We rehearsed this moment down at the river, so now we all step into the cave together. No tumbling, no bells, no whistles . . . just the soft light and the sound of the door closing behind us. Mary steps up onto the stone bench, but instead of walking to her left, she turns to her right—another point we rehearsed, regarding the room number we hope to find. My thinking is that every room in this 19th Palace has a key along the bench, so because we want to explore rooms 120 to 150, it makes sense we start in the opposite direction. Mary places her palms against the wall, moving slowly to her right. She quickly finds a glowing inscription but continues searching until she recognizes the Hebrew symbol for the numeral 120. I see beads of perspiration glistening on her forehead as she places her right palm over the glowing inscription, and I hear gasps of astonishment as a portal opens under her hand. Knowing the drill, she quickly gestures the portal open with her left hand then steps through the doorway.

Elizabeth, John, and Eric follow her into room 120 before Carol and I also step into the room. The bronze plaque on the door explains we are actually in a hallway of many linked rooms through this doorway: 120–134. Having noted the grouping of these rooms, Mary recognizes an opportunity to present important information to John and Elizabeth: "You need a little history for this next section of 15 rooms." The teenagers stop their fascinated exploration of the room to listen to their mother. "Each room was constructed as an excellent example of praise and teaching, to recite and sing, to memorize and review as the King's children and their families went up to worship the King once a year—they would march to a city set on a hill, the same sacred place mentioned in room 22 of the

The King's 19th Palace

Genesis Palace, one of seven small mountains in Jerusalem. Each of the rooms in this wing of the 19th Palace is called a Psalm or Song of Ascent, and all are marching songs based on two central themes—teaching the King's Word and remembrance."

Elizabeth and John absorb this information with interest, but John has a question: "Is it on Mount Zion, Mom? The sacred city on a hill?"

"Yes, John, it is. The sacred city is mentioned many times throughout the construction of the palaces of this Kingdom." Mary catches my eye, and we smile as her children continue exploring with renewed vigor.

"So put on a pair of virtual-reality specs and get ready for your teaching and singing session!" I recall the marching videos in some of our previous rooms. All have prepared me to fall smartly into step with the King's marching army, but only now do I realize I am marching with all the other righteous, chosen children through the ages. We are marching upward, ascending to the gates of the Kingdom, to go through the gates, to Zion, the holy hill of His dwelling. Together we pass along the path through the rooms, singing in each the words written, streaming, dancing, in holograms, in streaking beams of light, and projected literally right in front of our eyes—but for your benefit, allow me to paraphrase a few of my favorite phrases or parts of the songs of praise we are singing: "Too long I have had my dwelling place among those who hate peace and instead want war"; "I lift my eyes to the hills, knowing my help comes from the King. He is my keeper and watches over me"; "I was glad when I was told we will go to the house of the King, inside the very gates, the place of peace and not of war."

Having joined my family in song, along with the celestial choir and all the saints through the ages, we continue on, singing words to the next song: "If it had not been for the King on my side, where would I be?" The answer is clear: I would have been swallowed up in the darkness, swept away in a flood. Instead, we can trust in our

King in His holy city upon His holy hill called Mount Zion. We all join our voices again to sing, "He surrounds us with songs of deliverance" while we march onward and upward. Each song we sing together is also teaching our children to rely on the King's Word: "The King has done great things for us; we are glad." We see what we sowed with tears and weeping, we are now reaping with joy, as we sing, "Bringing in the Sheaves." He helps us as we build—indeed we can only build because of the ability He has given us—as each of us sees the house we grew up in being built, followed by ourselves being put as living stones in a temple-like building being constructed.

He watches over us and our children. We are blessed when we follow the King and walk in His directed paths. All you must do is seek the righteous path, and you shall find it. We are sorrowful for those who have not been chosen and do not choose to march with us, but at the same time we're thankful *our* cry from the depths was heard, resulting in the King's mercy on each of us *who believes*. He has removed our sin and adopted us as His children. I continue to wait on my King just as the watchman of the night waits for the morning light. The King is the One with steadfast love, who redeemed me—He is my hope. I have a quiet and calm soul, yet I have an excited spirit within as I enter through the gates to sing praises to my King for all He has done and will continue to do forever. My heart is glad to be in this place the King has chosen to dwell—where I now dwell. In unity, we all dwell here, a place with the feeling of precious anointing oil on my head, like sparkling dewdrops collecting together to form a gentle stream, running down from the mountain to become a river—a place of life forevermore! So as we reach the house of the King, we stand and lift our hands and bless our King.

I circle back to stop again in room 127, and my eyes are drawn to a multimedia presentation. The first image being shown is a tree laden with fruit. Men and women are eating the fruit, but then the tree is chopped down, leaving only a stump. I watch as a shoot starts rising from the stump, quickly becoming a full-grown tree again. Then a calendar appears, showing days and seasons passing by in the background, and as I encircle the tree, I see fruit appearing in turn on the branches in each season. A new image appears, and I see a white robe changing to red then to purple and back to a brilliant and blinding white. I see people appearing, each being clothed in a white robe with ever-increasing brightness. I see my own clothes fall away, and the white robe of His righteousness encircles me as the brightness intensifies. I see less and less of myself until finally, I only know I am still present by feeling and pinching myself. This is the opposite of the darkness I once experienced, where I also could not perceive or see anything, but now it is so different. I have a sense of many things, including my previous record of a similar sequence. The image changes yet again, and I see another tree that I somehow know is a family tree, with the cycle I have seen before.

I see a cycle of life continuing as the tree buds and grows leaves. The leaves mature then turn color and die, dropping to the ground but still identifiable as individual leaves. The leaves then start decaying, returning to the soil that nourishes the next generation of leaves. As the cycles continue, I realize images of my forbears are on the leaves, then I see myself, my wife and children, their spouses, my grandchildren and great-grandchildren. Continuing these cycles, I see foster sons, their siblings, those grandchildren, then my stepchildren and families, and so many more people I have known and shared life with. I have a sense of extreme gratitude and thankfulness as I see my heritage unfolding through all generations.

I desire to be a full and flourishing leaf all of my life, influencing coming generations who will not see or know me. It is not about me—*I want them to know the King!* Another scene unfolds with wheat growing, harvested, then crushed and the chaff blown away. Bread is prepared, and I dip it in red liquid before I eat, remembering all the King has done, is doing, and will do for me! A cup of living water from an adjacent river is given to me to drink. Then the scene changes again, and I see behind the river a city unlike the cities of doom and gloom on the outside. Instead, it is a city with many beautiful houses, streets of gold, and this broad, beautiful river flowing toward me from the center.

We spend many hours exploring the wonders of these 15 rooms, and although we have not completely mined the wealth of information they contain, we decide to continue our journey through the 19th Palace. We still have on our glasses as we enter room 135, and the first thing I notice is I am no longer marching with all the King's children. Instead I am now standing in the house of the King, praising the King's name and His goodness. I'm experiencing a pleasant feeling as I sing praises to His name for having chosen me. For a fleeting moment I see, yet again, the idols of silver and gold substituting for a king in the outside kingdoms. *What a great King we have! He is above all others, and we bless His name.* I leave this room expecting to enter the next in numerical sequence, but then I remember rooms 136–139 were connected to room 92, which we have previously visited. Instead, we are about to enter room 140.

We enter this final complex of ten rooms, which are also connected. My family—all with glasses still on—start slowly exploring, but I quickly move through them all, soon realizing the rooms have been built in a complete, seemingly unending circle looking inward to the throne room of the King. I realize I am facing the front of the throne in every room around the complete circle. Never to a side, I am always front and center before that throne! In the twisted world, continually spinning, though I may be upside down relative to Mars or the Sun, amazingly and somehow I am always before and looking up to my King. Although each room is open to the universe around, virtually no one is turned or looking outward. I am now back to the first of these rooms where I find Eric and Elizabeth in the midst of a throng of people, singing with great

The King's 19th Palace

gusto—so I join them in praising our King: "Behold, the King is upon His throne. I used to wander kingdoms of my own, but now I follow my King alone. To Him my hands I raise, Him to thank and praise." I give myself over to the joyous worship of our King—I sit, I stand, I sing, I praise, I dance! I never could dance well; clapping and raising my hands—or shouting in joy—also was always difficult, but I am changing.

As if to emphasize how much I have changed in the King's service, I take up various musical instruments—first a French horn (the only one I ever played besides the piano)—playing all of them vigorously as I join in with the joyous throng in worshipping the King before His throne. We have arrived at His house on Mount Zion! I have longed for this moment, where all the King's children can freely enter in to give the King all the praise and glory due His name. *Everything within my entire being worships the King.* We are considered righteous by the King and have the privilege of dwelling in His presence. Our prayers are like incense rising to Him. I give Him thanks as I change seamlessly from one room to the next. During the times I sit, I am reminded of all the King has done. His creation, His saving me from my sin and protecting me from all evil. His causing me all the more to praise and thank Him for lifting me up from the miry pit, delivering me from my enemies. His teaching me to do His will and to proclaim to others exactly who my King is—and what His salvation ultimately means for all of us.

As He did for me, He saves those who have fallen, who have been muddied and hurt by sin, and He even saves those who have harbored hate in their hearts toward the King. He has chosen His children out of the world and its ways. While assigning me to speak of His love to people outside this Kingdom, He properly trained me for battle, down to my very fingers. I will endure any suffering, having become a good and properly trained soldier. *He is the source of life and breath and everything that is. He is my Rock and Refuge.* He has blessed me thoroughly, enabling me to now be a blessing and servant to Him. I will bless and praise Him forever in this place. I join with all creation in praising, honoring, and exalting the name of the King. He reigns in majesty.

I leave Eric and Elizabeth in room 143 and continue exploring, stopping for a long while in room 145. Here I am reminded of all the King has taught me to say and do, especially when next I travel outside as an alien and sojourner to share His good news. As I pause in room 147, I see a table prepared and a cornucopia full. I am reminded to be thankful for all His abundant provision—He declares and it is done, provided by His Word. Now I see snow as a covering like wool and hail He sends like morsels of food. I do not want to remain as cold as ice—instead, I contemplate His Word melting the ice within me. In rooms 148 and 149, I stop to marvel toward the place of my glorious King, in His heights. I hear music, singing, and praise, and when I look carefully, I can make out an old rugged cross at the base of a distant hill. I have seen it from a closer vantage point in some of the King's other palaces, and I long for the day you see it, too, although it is only a hint right now. When I survey that wondrous cross, I am reminded of my absolute gain and the hope I have of the eternal life promised to me. Just like you, that cross is a reminder of what the King's Son did in sacrificing Himself for us, a realization of what I now have been given after the King's Spirit transplanted a new heart within me.

I know this: in the fullness of time, the King sent His Son, so He could suffer in my place then lead me into the Kingdom. *What amazing and steadfast love the King has for you and me!* Just the mention of the King's name reminds me of His strength, so I start singing, "He is like a strong tower and has all the power." His steadfast love protects me, covers me, and surrounds me securely forever! Then some of the lyrics to another song: "Blessed be Your name in all this land. In the darkness, You are light. Walking in suffering, You relieve the pain." You have changed my heart. You have poured Your Living Water upon me, and it rises like a spring within me.

The King's 19th Palace

I see movement from the corner of my eye, and when I turn to look, I see Eric and Carol enter the room. Then together we sing, "How marvelous, how wonderful, is the King's love for me." Mary, John, and Elizabeth enter opposite, and yet another song floods over me, which we all sing together: "Revive Us Again." It reminds me of the ending of a play when all the cast comes together on what is now this stage of life.

I am utterly grateful to be sharing this moment—this part—with my precious family, and I rejoice fervently. I have been told the word *rejoice* means "surrounding or encircling in joyous celebration," which I think is still another reason for these rooms to encircle the King's dwelling, all facing before Him as He sits on His throne. What a joy to join the procession and gathering as we also form a circle. What the King has done in us *can and will* happen in others. I used to follow the laws of the kingdoms outside, but now I am under the rules of the place of my new citizenship. I have become an ambassador.

Even though we are in a wing of the palace that encompasses the King's throne room, I still see some reminders, right before my eyes. I cannot help but glimpse outward, seeing the evil continuing outside the gates. My King is the overwhelming fire of heat and light, a fire that is consuming and at the same time purifying, destroying forever those who have become utterly useless—having chosen evil—while making the rest pure for His use, removing all our dross. I see myself as an ember of a smoking wick being fanned into flame. The smoke disappears as I burn brightly and reflect the light of the King! His heat and light overwhelm me for my good and His glory. I am used, not useless. I am being purified and refined by His fire, not consumed. I have light and see my path; I am not blinded or flailing in the dark. I cannot wait for the day when all work for Him is completed and the King tells each of us, "Well done, my faithful servant, enter into the joy of your Master." What a glorious forever, this dwelling place in the very presence of our King, serving and worshipping Him while evermore learning the finer details of His glory. *Let everything and everyone sing praises to the Lord!*

We make our way back to the overhang, thrilled at what we have experienced. The stars are shining brightly in the heavens above, so we make a fire under the overhang and continue talking late into the night. The fire and the stars overhead provide us with an excellent reminder of the Light of the world we will one day see face-to-face in the brightness we can only imagine.

We speak in hushed tones about our mighty King, who is also our Cornerstone and Capstone, the One who holds us and molds us. He is our Master Architect and Builder, refining each of His precious, living stones, shaping us to fit the space He specifically created for each of us before the foundation of the earth. As for me and my household, we will serve our King, grateful to be a vibrant part of His eternal house.

Psalm 130 is one of the rooms reminding us that God our King not only chose us, but He rescued us. He brought us up out of the pit of miry clay (that sinful state that keeps us from standing), putting our feet on His solid Rock. Through His Son He redeemed us by His sacrifice, saving us from our sins.

Epilogue

Hear words of truth, remembering to build your own house on the solid Rock. You are that house you, then you can withstand the storms of earthly life (based on Matthew 7:24–25).

First, I must tell you I have taken nearly all my family and extended family on journeys to parts of our physical world, as well as like a docent to "visit" various—and for some family members all—of the 66 palaces in the Kingdom. In this account, I have been given the privilege of taking you on a journey of exploration and discovery within the rooms in this awe-inspiring 19th Palace of the King, through which the physical and spiritual examples of the admixture of stone, wood, and valuable metals have reflected the values, teachings, and promises spoken by the King through His Word, recorded by His servants. These rooms, built with a range of materials and furnished in diverse ways, provide a reflection of worldly and spiritual concepts. I have depicted these concepts using words that describe different media methods, including song, film, and virtual-reality descriptions that, ultimately, are all an attempt to reflect the values, teachings, and promises spoken by the King.

Second, note, not a single room was empty! Each and every visit provided something to observe, hear, perceive, then apply.

And there is always the unseen spiritual Presence in each room to help with your vision, understanding, thoughts, application, and emotions.

Third, the Guidebook mentioned is of course the Bible, which we know is the expressed Word of God directed by His Spirit upon chosen men (we speak of the inspiration of the Scriptures, so what God breathed out was taken in then written down). This Guidebook is not only for our reading, understanding, and application, but it also is the truth to be shared with others. Romans 10:8–20 teaches us the Word is near us and in our hearts, and we are called not only to confess that Jesus is the way, the truth, and the life, but we are to be the feet to go and tell others that truth and good news.

Our journey hopefully has revealed how our King's plan—to incorporate His chosen family members into a living edifice that He and they can all call home—was generated before the foundation of the earth. The King's master plan—to build His house comprised of living stones—has always been under construction and continues to this day, using each of His chosen and adopted children to fit into their eternal piece and place of His house as living stones, built upon that sure and solid Cornerstone (who is also the Capstone).

Is that a click of the tongue I hear? An objection to the term *our King*? I use this term because *God is the Architect of the universe and everything within it,* whether or not an individual accepts His lordship. We all want a leader to take charge, until we have one!

You see, an individual's refusal to acknowledge God cannot alter the basic truth of His sovereignty over all of creation. The Bible makes this clear to us. Matthew, speaking of the Father who is in heaven, plainly stated, "For He makes His sun rise on the evil and on the good, and sends rain on the just and on the unjust." The King provides for everyone alike, but those who are chosen to join His family receive the added blessing of intimacy with Him. It is this intimacy I wanted to depict as we journeyed together through this fascinating landscape, exploring this particular palace, where the architecture and furnishings of each room reflect the essence of the living Word, influencing us to learn and apply His truth to every aspect of our lives as we grasp the value of serving Him.

The grand architecture of the magnificent palace we have visited is but one of 66 beautifully crafted buildings the King spoke into being, which, as we have seen, all share the same Cornerstone—even though human builders initially rejected this vital and pivotal foundation of every building within the Father's Kingdom. You might think, *How is that even possible? How can 66 separate buildings all share the same Cornerstone?* When fully explored, this question reveals the powerful and captivating metaphor upon which this book is built. Allow me to elaborate. The Bible teaches us God is omnipresent, meaning He is everywhere at the same time, as well as outside of time restraints. The Bible combines a rich pattern of symbolic and other multiple forms of meaning woven through the 66 books of which it is comprised, and within this pattern is a specific correlation equating both God the Father and God the Son with a *Rock*. We have explored the meaning of this symbolism in ever-greater detail as we progressed through the rooms of the King's awe-inspiring 19th Palace—the one building we have visited, explored, and on which we have focused.

The book of Psalms (the King's awe-inspiring 19th Palace) was written over a thousand-year period, and King David—who wrote most of these psalms—elegantly summed up the essence of this conceptual image: "I love you, O Lord, my strength. *The Lord is my rock* and my fortress and my deliverer, *my God, my rock*, in whom I take refuge, my shield, and the horn of my salvation, my stronghold" (Psalm 18:1–2, my emphasis). Notice how this passage fluctuates between the latent potential for protection encapsulated within the inanimate structures (*rock, fortress, shield, stronghold*) and those dynamic and animated qualities imbued with the active protection God offers—He was David's *strength* and his *deliverer*, his God in whom he took *refuge* and who was the power of his *salvation*. King David's understanding of the almighty God he served is reflected in this balance between his passive acceptance of God as his fortress of protection, and David's active engagement with God's power to ensure he walked in His strength and granted salvation.

The prophet Isaiah also made reference to this image of God as a solid foundation we can trust through eternity: "Trust in the Lord forever, for the Lord God is an *everlasting rock*" (Isaiah 26:4, my emphasis).

How then does this reference to the Father being an everlasting Rock relate to the Cornerstone upon which every book of the Bible is based? Let's explore several Scriptures together, so we can gain an understanding of how a single Cornerstone can form the critical foundation point of 66 different buildings and their rooms. We will begin by reading the opening verses of John's Gospel:

> In the beginning was the Word, and the Word was with God, and the Word was God. He was in the beginning with God. *All things were made through Him, and without Him was not any thing made that was made.* In Him was life, and the life was the light of men. The light shines in the darkness, and the darkness has not overcome it. (John 1:1–5, my emphasis)

As we keep reading John's Gospel, it becomes clear the "Word" in whom we find life and light is Jesus Christ, the only begotten Son of God. The salient point in this passage emphasizes *all* things—every tangible construct found on earth, both animate and inanimate—are made through Him . . . not a *single* thing that exists is created without the Son of God. This points directly to

Jesus as the Architect of the universe and all matter within it, and also reveals all life and light emanate out of Him. The apostle Peter grasped this revelation, so when Jesus asked him, "'But who do you say that I am?' Simon Peter replied, 'You are the Christ, the Son of the living God.'"[13]

Upon This Rock I Will Build My Church

Jesus not only acknowledged this revelation the Father gave to Peter; He also assured the apostle He would build His Church on the Rock of this revelation, and that Rock is the Christ, the Son of the living God. These prophetic words Jesus spoke pronounced the imminent fulfillment of the Father's master plan—the creation of a new family based on the bedrock of His only begotten Son, Jesus, designated the chief Cornerstone (and at the same time the Capstone holding all things together) even before the very foundation of the earth had been cast: "He was foreknown before the foundation of the world but was made manifest in the last times for the sake of you who through Him are believers in God, who raised Him from the dead and gave Him glory, so that your faith and hope are in God" (1 Peter 1:20–21).

A Cornerstone in Zion

Thus the psalmist, a prophet, an apostle, and the Messiah Himself all made reference to this chief Cornerstone who is the Rock and foundation upon which the 66 "buildings" and surrounding universe of the Father's entire Kingdom rests.

Psalmist

"The stone that the builders rejected has become the cornerstone" (Psalm 118:22).

---

13. Matthew 16:15b–16

Prophet

Spoken by the prophet Isaiah:

> [T]herefore thus says the Lord God, "Behold, I am the one who has laid as a foundation in Zion, a stone, a tested stone, a precious cornerstone, of a sure foundation: 'Whoever believes will not be in haste.' And I will make justice the line, and righteousness the plumb line." (Isaiah 28:16–17a)

Apostle

The apostle Peter was given clear insight into ancient prophecy and how it was being revealed before his eyes, expressing the radical truth that followers of Christ are both living stones and a holy priesthood:

> "As you come to Him, *a living stone* rejected by men but in the sight of God chosen and precious, *you yourselves like living stones are being built up as a spiritual house,* to be a holy priesthood, to offer spiritual sacrifices acceptable to God through Jesus Christ. For it stands in Scripture:
>
> 'Behold, I am laying in Zion a stone,
> *a cornerstone chosen and precious,*
> and whoever believes in Him will not be put to shame.'
>
> So the honor is for you who believe, but for those who do not believe,
>
> 'The stone (Jesus Christ) that the builders rejected
>   has become the cornerstone,' and
>
> 'A stone of stumbling,
>   and a rock of offense.'

They stumble because they disobey the word, as they were destined to do." 1 Peter 2:4–8 (my emphasis and parentheses inserted)

Messiah

While Jesus was teaching in the temple one day, the chief priests and the elders asked Him, "By what authority are you doing these things, and who gave you this authority?"[14] Jesus no doubt perceived their impure intention to trap Him, so He responded with a question of His own concerning whether the baptism of John came from heaven or from man. The priests and elders quickly realized whichever answer they gave would offend either God or the people, so they pleaded ignorance to the question. Jesus did not answer the question they had posed, providing them instead with two parables. At this point the Pharisees were also listening to what Jesus was saying, which becomes evident at the close of the chapter. Both parables essentially relate to those who are given an opportunity to either obey or disobey God—and through the use of parables, Jesus had them understand that disobedience to God is deserving of "a miserable death."[15]

Jesus then went on to reference the stone the builders rejected becoming the cornerstone, having first brought clarity and meaning to the image of the rejected cornerstone through the parables He had just told, concerning disobedience:

> Jesus said to them, "Have you never read in the Scriptures:
>
> "'The stone that the builders rejected
>   has become the cornerstone;
> this was the Lord's doing,
>   and it is marvelous in our eyes'?

---

14. Matthew 21:23b
15. Portion of, and based on Matthew 21:41

> Therefore I tell you, the kingdom of God will be taken away from you and given to a people producing its fruits. And the one who falls on this stone will be broken to pieces; and when it falls on anyone, it will crush him."
>
> When the chief priests and the Pharisees heard His parables, they perceived that He was speaking about them. And although they were seeking to arrest Him, they feared the crowds, because they held Him to be a prophet.[16]

This is the wisdom we expect from the Messiah! Knowing the wicked intentions of their hearts, He countered them with the Word of God, just as He had countered Satan with the Word while in the wilderness at the start of His ministry. Having established who this chief Cornerstone is—the Rock upon which the weight of the Father's entire Kingdom rests—we also delve into yet another mystery: by what power is the Father's Kingdom held together?

Those who seek assurance of the supremacy of God's Son need look no further than the first chapter of Hebrews:

> Long ago, at many times and in many ways, God spoke to our fathers by the prophets, but in these last days He has spoken to us by his Son, whom He appointed the heir of all things, *through whom also He created the world.* He is the radiance of the glory of God and the exact imprint of His nature, *and He upholds the universe by the word of His power."* Hebrews 1:1–3a (my emphasis)

---

16. Matthew 21:42–46

Jesus Christ not only "created the world," but in addition to this, He "upholds the universe by the word of His power." The apostle Paul was also aware of Christ being the Cornerstone of His church. Much like Peter, however, he took this analogy one step further and explained how all the saints are growing into a holy temple built on the foundation of the apostles and prophets, with Jesus being the Cornerstone:

> For through Him [Jesus] we both have access in one Spirit to the Father. So then you are no longer strangers and aliens, but you are fellow citizens with the saints and members of the household of God, built on the foundation of the apostles and prophets, Christ Jesus Himself being the Cornerstone, in whom the whole structure, *being joined together, grows into a holy temple in the Lord.* In Him you also are being built together into a dwelling place for God by the Spirit. (Ephesians 2:18–22, my addition and emphasis)

Both Peter and Paul recognized and understood that those who willingly choose to serve and obey God are living stones in the process of being formed into a living temple, in which the Spirit of God will reside throughout eternity. As we have explored the rooms of the 19th Palace on our journey, we have begun to understand how our King's plan, present before the foundation of the earth, is being slowly yet methodically brought into existence throughout the ages, and in each of His children!

The most crucial aspect of any construction is its foundation—everything that follows is at risk if the cornerstone is weak or faulty. For this reason, the cornerstone not only is first to direct the exact alignment but also must be tried and tested to give us the surety the resulting building is built correctly and will not crack nor crumble.

Matthew 4 gives us some insight into the manner in which the devil tried and tested Jesus when He was led by the Spirit into the wilderness. Three times Jesus refuted Satan's attempts to overcome Him by quoting Scripture to this wicked fallen angel. There are many more examples of how Jesus proved to everyone who had ears to hear that He was the precious, tested Cornerstone foretold by the prophet Isaiah, and some of these examples became apparent as we journeyed through the King's awe-inspiring 19th Palace.

As fascinating as this may be, what is the overarching point being presented to us through God's Word? Paul, in his epistle to the Corinthian church, gave us an excellent assessment of how we are to take part in the process of building ourselves as God's living temple:

> "He who plants and he who waters are one, and each will receive his wages according to his labor. For we are God's fellow workers. You are God's field, God's building.
>
> According to the grace of God given to me, like a skilled master builder I laid a foundation, and someone else is building upon it. *Let each one take care how he builds upon it.* For no one can lay a foundation other than that which is laid, which is Jesus Christ. Now if anyone builds on the foundation with gold, silver, precious stones, wood, hay, straw—each one's work will become manifest, for the Day will disclose it, because it will be revealed by fire, and the fire will test what sort of work each one has done. If the work that anyone has built on the foundation survives, he will receive a reward. If anyone's work is burned up, he will suffer loss, though he himself will be saved, but only as through fire.

> Do you not know that you are God's temple and that God's Spirit dwells in you? If anyone destroys God's temple, God will destroy him. For God's temple is holy, and you are that temple." 1 Corinthians 3:8–17, my emphasis

This passage tells us in greater detail how we are meant to follow Christ the Cornerstone by building and being built on this unshakable foundation He laid, just as all the saints who went before and all the current souls being added as living stones.

Having now gained a better understanding of how Christ the Cornerstone underpins every book of the Bible—every one of the 66 palaces He has constructed—I suggest you journey once more (at least) through this beautiful 19th Palace and every other palace crafted by the King. By revisiting the King's 19th Palace, your comprehension of His steadfast love will undoubtedly grow, while your exploration of the other 65 palaces will reveal to you the importance of applying *all* His precepts to your daily life.

New Jerusalem

If I were to write in a similar manner about all the other buildings of His Kingdom, or if I were a docent taking you through all the rooms, I would first ask if the King's Spirit has changed your heart—so you, too, may become an adopted child of the King. On any tour, I would have you pray then enter and explore each room on your own, coming out to share your observations and understanding. Then I would repeatedly share with you the joy of knowing Him as your Lord and King. At the end of our extensive time together, I would complete each visit of seeing His truth by reflecting upon only a portion thereof, as I might see in my mind or with those virtual-reality glasses:

> I am invited in through the gate, and I see a sprawling complex of exquisite buildings spread out before me. Thousands of fellow citizens glow as shiny facets of light and delight, each reflecting back into my shining eyes and I am enrapt with wonder. I am led into the nearest building, taken upstairs, and led onto an outside balcony where I take in the vast metropolis of the King's Kingdom. I am utterly astounded at the attention to detail carved into every aspect of each building, and my senses drink in the beauty of the landscape. I recognize what must be the River of Life and the Tree of Life set in the center of all these striking structures. The streets are paved with gold, and the buildings are built upon precious stones that also shimmer with the reflected light of the King....[17]

The paragraph above gives us a sneak preview of what is to come—in some manner, a beautiful, futuristic city is what we have to look forward to at the end of our earthly journey. To all those who have embraced the King and who are already acquainted with the 66 buildings comprising God's interactive message of truth to humanity throughout the ages, each of you will have a mansion room in this city, and your name will appear in the King's Book of Life.

---

17. Author's thoughts

Afterword

This 19th Palace and its 150 rooms has not only been a pleasant place to experience both learning and teaching, but has also been a training platform to apply our knowledge and understanding of the King's message. It is an excellent example of how He prepares you and me to share, using the abilities and gifts He has granted us in such rich supply. Even though His Kingdom is a comfortable, safe, and protected place, I also was given the awesome privilege of sharing His message in the outside kingdoms. I am so thankful for this and all the other palaces, which have had an incalculable effect on my life through their teachings, refining and increasing my spiritual maturity.

I know I can count on the presence of the King's Spirit to help keep me from returning to sin, temptation, and evil, as well as protecting me against other assaults on my faith while doing His work. Thankfully, I can also count on His Spirit to bring me back to this Kingdom—to reside forever in a room prepared for me in His dwelling place. What has sometimes felt like forced growth, as well as firm teaching to understand and apply, I now see is really the overarching or capstone effects of His steadfast love, shown to me in every aspect of my life. He has taught me to walk properly and to know I am still a traveler on His directed journey.

The King's 19th Palace

I want to tell you about one more memory from my childhood. I grew up helping my dad raise cattle, and many times I had to round them up. About once a year, we branded the cattle, which meant heating up our "Y box" branding iron in a fire then quickly searing the hide of the animal, resulting in a permanent identifying mark—somewhat similar to a tattoo. This identifying mark signified the branded animal was ours. In my training within the various Kingdom palaces, I was fascinated by the account in the Zechariah Palace, room 3, about our being chosen by the King, rescued and removed from the fire—hot but not consumed. Just like this charred log or brand rescued from sin and death, we too now have the capacity to transfer the King's mark to others—like my using a branding iron in my youth. The description then continues to tell of filthy garments being removed and replaced by clean, kingly garments. Not only are we the brand plucked from the fire, but we are also newly clothed—and our heated branding iron is to be used to brand others. We have been changed by our King, given knowledge and understanding, but we are also charged with imprinting His message upon others.

I could tell you so much more than these few noted *items* from my study and application of each psalm and for all the other palaces and their rooms, but enough for now. I do encourage you to visit all of them. You will be amazed at the great love the King has for you, especially as you learn more of the truth His Word encompasses and as you apply His precepts to your minute-by-minute, second-by-second walk. Your walk may be on varied terrain: while you are in His Kingdom studying and meditating in the various rooms you visit, or when you are on a special pilgrimage and mission outside. May you walk worthy individually, with others, or serving in His army. Just as He rescued you and me as a brand from the fire, He is using you in His branding business!

Whether through a short conversation or a long time of ministry, you will have the privilege of encouraging others to believe in the King, and to take in His truth and His promises, enabling them to live fulfilled lives as His adopted children.

This book was written for those of my family and friends—present and future—who desire to explore the King's Palace and learn how *their* stone is or can be built upon the Cornerstone.

About the Author

Dr. Gene Baillie is a retired physician living in Greenville, SC, and Salem, OR. He grew up in rural Nebraska, the oldest of six children and the first member of his family to attend college. He and his first wife, Gini, were married for 51 years before her death in 2015 from the brain cancer glioblastoma. Now married to Carol, they have a combined family that includes five daughters, four foster sons, eleven grandchildren, and seven great-grandchildren.

Gene encourages people to read and study the Bible, so your house will be built on Christ the solid Rock and Cornerstone. He is an elder in the Presbyterian Church in America and the author of five other books, all described and available at ReadGoodBooks.org or by searching the author's name on Google or Amazon. The titles are *The Journey Home*, *Nothing Matters*, *Death Takes Time*, *Walk with Me*, and *Beyond the Bottle*. An "Eternal Blueprint" gospel presentation (answers for the three problems of a bad heart, bad record, and bad life) as well Bible study notes are available by contacting the author at GeneBaillie@gmail.com.

Gene Baillie Publishing LLC
ReadGoodBooks.org

www.ingramcontent.com/pod-product-compliance
Lightning Source LLC
Chambersburg PA
CBHW051546010526
44118CB00022B/2596